Meeting Mr. Lincoln

Long ABRAHAM LINCOLN a Little Longer.

Meeting Mr. Lincoln

Firsthand Recollections of Abraham Lincoln
by People, Great and Small,
Who Met the President

EDITED WITH AN INTRODUCTION AND NOTES BY
VICTORIA RADFORD

Ivan R. Dee
Chicago 1998

MEETING MR. LINCOLN. Copyright © 1998 by Victoria Radford.
All rights reserved, including the right to reproduce this book or
portions thereof in any form. For information, address: Ivan R. Dee,
Publisher, 1332 North Halsted Street, Chicago 60622. Manufactured
in the United States of America and printed on acid-free paper.

Library of Congress Cataloging-in-Publication Data:
Meeting Mr. Lincoln : firsthand recollections of Abraham Lincoln by
    people, great and small, who met the president / edited with an
    introduction and notes by Victoria Radford.
        p.   cm.
    Includes bibliographical references and index.
    ISBN 1-56663-199-8 (acid-free paper)
    1. Lincoln, Abraham, 1809–1865—Anecdotes.   2. Lincoln,
Abraham, 1809–1865—Friends and associates—Anecdotes.
I. Radford, Victoria, 1966–
E457.15.M44   1998
973.7'092—dc21   98-24074

For Elvis and Teague

Contents

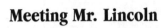

Meeting Mr. Lincoln

Introduction

THIS BOOK is about what it would have been like to meet President Abraham Lincoln in person. Imagine walking into the White House between 1861 and 1865. What kind of access would you have found to the president? Had you gone to meet him, with no accolades to your name, no titles, would he have received you and talked with you? Had you seen him, would you have formed a favorable impression of his dignity, intelligence, and character? Or would the visit have reinforced the contemporary popular view of Lincoln as uneducated and uncouth?

Imagine you are a young girl, like India Francis Brown, whose husband has been captured by Union forces and is being held as a spy at Old Capitol Prison in Washington, facing possible execution. Your only hope is to go to Washington and somehow intercede for him, but whom you will see or what exactly you will do is unclear. All you know is that you are alive and have your freedom, and your husband is facing death. You know that your husband is not a spy, you know that he and his comrades had simply fallen behind their company through weariness and exhaustion and had been discovered seeking shelter in the woods. You go to the prison where your husband is being held and are turned away. You go to see Secretary of War Edwin Stanton and are gruffly told to leave. Your only remaining hope is to see the president himself. The idea of going to see the President of the United States scares you, for you do not know if you can even get in to see him, and if you can, you do not know if he will take the time to listen to you. After all, you are only a common citizen, and a Confederate at that. You are afraid he will turn you away, tell you to stop wasting his time. You have heard hard things about this president. You have heard he is a tyrant, you have heard him called a baboon, an idiot, a scoundrel. But you know he is your last hope.

You know that the White House is open to the public and that Lincoln, on most days, will admit visitors. When you arrive at the steps of the White House you tell the doorkeeper you wish to see the president. You are ushered in to a massive waiting room, full of all types of people. Some you guess are senators or congressmen, men who appear dignified and seem irritated to be kept waiting; others look like businessmen, expectant and nervous. A few women are there, some well dressed, some not. Visitors are called in to see the president one by one, but your name is not called. You are told to come back the next day.

After waiting several days to see the president, you are finally ushered into Lincoln's office and left alone with the lean, gaunt, somewhat haggard-looking figure of the president towering over you. In your arms is your infant daughter, whom you held against your chest as you traveled in a flat-bottom boat, under cover of night, risking your own life as you traveled the heavily blockaded waters between Alexandria and Washington. Lincoln smiles, puts you in a chair, and asks, "What can I do for you?" His kindness, after all you have been through, is too much, and your eyes fill with tears. But you begin to tell your story, and Lincoln listens intently, sometimes smiling and sometimes rubbing his chin. When you are finished, you are crying, and Lincoln holds your baby for a moment to help you pull yourself together, lifting her up in his arms and holding her close against his cheeks. When you are calm, he hands the baby back to you and writes something on a piece of paper. Handing the paper to you, he says, "Take this to Secretary Stanton, Mrs. Brown. If what you say is true, your husband will be returned to you." As you get up to leave, Lincoln says, "Mrs. Brown, you are a brave little woman," and then he opens the door for you. You leave, too shocked and elated to say anything. Three days later your husband is discharged from prison, emaciated and trembling with nerves and fever. When he recovers somewhat, you tell him of the debt of gratitude you owe to Abraham Lincoln. Your husband says nothing but only hides his face in the pillows and cries.

This account of meeting President Lincoln is one of many. Scores of individuals met Abraham Lincoln in person and recorded their impressions. Time permitting, Lincoln would receive almost everyone who wished to see him. He met with people of all classes, sometimes passing over a waiting congressman or dignitary in favor of a private citizen, especially when one needed his help. He said this was one of the few things that made him happy—to know that he had helped someone. As he told his friend Joshua Speed, "Die when I may, I want it said of me by those who know me best to say that I always plucked a thistle and planted a flower when I thought a flower would grow. . . ."

Swarms of visitors arrived early in the morning at the White House and would stay all day waiting for a chance to talk with the president. Senators and congressmen came to see him to discuss political matters, office-seekers to ask for a new post or promotion, generals and admirals to discuss the war, inventors to discuss their inventions, social activists to plead their causes, ordinary citizens to ask for help or just to meet the president in person. There were so many visitors, and Lincoln was so determined to see them, that John George Nicolay and John Hay, his personal secretaries, estimated that Lincoln, at least in the early years of his administration, spent three-quarters of his time with visitors. His secretaries begged him to set limits. At first he agreed to limit his office hours to sixteen a week, but then he proceeded to, as Hay put it, "break through every regulation as fast as it was made." If his personal secretaries tried to tell anyone to come back during regular office hours, Lincoln would usually stick his head out of his office door and invite them in anyway. As he told his friend Henry Wilson, "They don't want much; they get but little, and I must see them."

Lincoln wasn't simply being eccentric; this was part of his democratic philosophy. He saw presidential contact with the people to be part of democracy, keeping the connection between citizens and their leader. When Josiah Blackburn, a reporter for the London *Free Press*, asked Lincoln why he did not hand the duty of meeting with so many people over to someone else, the president explained that "the office of President is essentially a civil one. . . . For myself, I feel—though the tax on my time is heavy—that no hours of my day are better employed than those which thus bring me again within the direct contact and atmosphere of the average of our whole people. Men moving only in an official circle are apt to become merely official—not to say arbitrary—in their ideas and are apter and apter, with each passing day, to forget that they only hold power in a representative capacity. Now this is all wrong. . . . Many of the matters brought to my notice are utterly frivolous, but others are of more or less importance, and all serve to renew in me a clearer and more vivid image of that great popular assemblage out of which I sprung, and to which at the end of two years I must return. I tell you . . . that I call these receptions my *'public opinion baths,'* for I have but little time to read the papers and gather public opinion that way; and though they may not be pleasant in all their particulars, the effect, as a whole is renovating and invigorating to my perceptions of responsibility and duty."

This book is a collection of actual firsthand accounts of meeting President Lincoln. In all of them, the people who met Abraham Lincoln found in some way a different man than they expected. Some people were surprised by his appearance, that this haphazard and untidy man was indeed president. Some were surprised at his generosity, that he would take the time to see them and listen to their stories. Some were surprised by his kindness, that he would offer help and kind words whenever he could. Some, like India Francis Brown, were surprised by his compassion and mercy, and some by his simple dignity and grace. And many were surprised at how *they* felt in Lincoln's presence, that his sincerity and ease of manner set them at *their* ease, so they forgot they were even talking with a president.

Part One

FIRST IMPRESSIONS

YOU ARE escorted into the White House's elegant and ornate Blue Room, where you wait with about fifty others. After about half an hour, a servant arrives to announce that the president is ready to receive visitors. You are ushered, with the rest of the crowd, into the president's small office. There is barely enough room for everyone present. The office is simple and utilitarian, the only adornment being a picture of Andrew Jackson that hangs above the fireplace. Within a few minutes the tall, lanky form of Mr. Lincoln walks in. His gait is unsteady. His left shoulder, slightly higher than his right, causes his walk to be undulating and slightly off balance. At either side of his towering figure, his long pendulous arms end in hands of extraordinary dimensions. His legs, too long for the rest of his body, end in feet of even more remarkable size. His attire, a simple black suit, is ill fitting and wrinkled; his rough, unmanageable hair stands out in every direction.

His face, it seems to you, is not at all appealing. The lips are too large, the face is bony, the ears protrude outward. The eyes, sunken under thick eyebrows, have a haggard, careworn look, and the skin is dark and rough. You are surprised at first that this awkward and untidy man could be president. He looks to you more like a country schoolmaster or day laborer. You think of how he has been characterized in the press—as a country hick, a simpleton who would prefer to spend his time telling stories, cracking jokes, and drinking whiskey. But as you look at him more closely you can see within the eyes an intelligence, a shrewdness, and you begin to see in his manners, despite their awkwardness, an essential dignity and poise.

"[A] flippant remark calculated to appeal to the vulgarian"

Alban Jasper Conant, assigned to paint a portrait of Lincoln shortly after the first presidential election, chats with Lincoln but misjudges his character.

PROMPTLY on the hour, Lincoln rose, came over, and without a word threw his angular form into the chair, crossing his legs and settling back with a sigh, as though to a disagreeable ordeal. Immediately his countenance relapsed into impenetrable abstraction; the hard, sinister lines deepened into an expression of utter melancholy, almost despair. The cold sweat started all over me as I contemplated the difficulty of inducing the animation I had observed the day before.

᾿ Something had to be done, and I began by asking permission to arrange his hair, which stood out like an ovenbroom. He nodded, and with my fingers I brushed it back, disclosing the splendid lines of the forehead. At least that was something, I thought, as I backed away. But it was not enough. All the other features seemed to me hopeless, as I stood there. His ill repute in my section flooded into my mind: his common origin—born of Kentucky "poor white

[From Alban Jasper Conant, "A Portrait Painter's Reminiscences of Lincoln," *McClure's* magazine, March 1909]

---

trash"; his plebeian pursuits, his coarse tastes and low associates. He seemed to me, indeed, the story-telling, whiskey-drinking, whiskey-selling country grocer who they said had been exalted to the exclusion of the astute Seward.

So, as I sat down again before my easel, I made some flippant remark calculated to appeal to the vulgarian. It was then I got my first hint of the innate dignity of the man. He made some monosyllabic reply, and there came over his face the most marvelously complex expression I have ever seen—a mingling of instant shrewd apprehension of the whole attitude of mind back of my remark, pained disappointment at my misunderstanding of him, and patient tolerance of it. In a flash, I saw I had made a mistake, though not till long afterward did I realize how gross a one. To cover my embarrassment I began at once to question him about the debates with Douglas, which had been fully published in the St. Louis papers.

"A serious air at times which almost borders on the solemn"

This article was written by Samuel R. Weed, a reporter for a St. Louis newspaper. While those around Lincoln see him as a jokester, Mr. Weed sees a more accurate view.

THE DAY and night with Abraham Lincoln of which I shall tell were the most important in his life and, in the tremendous consequences which ensued, the most important to the country at large. I refer to the 6th day of November, 1860, and to the night which followed it. This was election day—the day which made Abraham Lincoln President of the United States.

At that time I was connected with the press of St. Louis and was delegated to spend the day and night in Springfield, Illinois, the home of Mr. Lincoln. My special duty was to remain as near to Mr. Lincoln as possible and to prepare an account of such incidents as might be deemed interesting to the public in connection with his movements on that memorable day, which was to make his life a part of American history or retire him for a while at least from the public gaze.

I reached Springfield about ten o'clock in the morning

[From Samuel R. Weed, "Hearing the Election Returns with Lincoln," *New York Times*, February 14, 1932] and, armed with my credentials and letters of introduction, was soon in Mr. Lincoln's presence. I found him in a private room attached to the office of the Illinois Secretary of State, which he had occupied as sort of headquarters for several months. When I entered, he was chatting with three or four friends as calmly and as amiably as if he had started on a picnic. In this apartment he had received many of the men afterward distinguished in the councils of the nation and also on her battlefields. His manner was quiet, unaffected and gracious, and, when I informed him of my errand, he smiled and hoped I would manage to enjoy myself.

I shall not undertake to describe Mr. Lincoln's personal appearance. The pictures of him, then and now so well known, give a fair idea of how he looked. He was then, and always, pre-eminently a plain man. I cannot easily forget that he was tall and angular, or that he had pretty long legs, especially when they were elevated to the top of a stove, as he sat in a chair tipped backward. As I first saw him I could not justify the reports that were everywhere circulated about his lack of personal beauty.

On this day Mr. Lincoln was in one of his most amiable moods, but he did not jest or crack jokes (as his enemies charged was his daily habit) in discussing the perilous condition of the country. I thought then—and have not changed my mind since—that whatever humor or sense of humor there was in him came spontaneously and that if he had tried to be humorous he would have failed. . . .

There were many quaint sayings by Mr. Lincoln during the day in reply, or by way of repartee, to remarks made in his presence. The idea seemed general even among his intimate friends that it was the proper thing to provoke from him something funny by saying something in his presence which would be called "smart" or "witty" and call forth a witty reply. Most of these attempts were decided failures. . . . One of his few humorous remarks was that it was lucky for him that "the women couldn't vote"; otherwise the monstrous portraits of him which had been circulated . . . by friends as well as by foes would surely defeat him.

. . . There was a constant stream of good nature in all of his sayings that day. His good nature never deserted him, and yet underneath I thought I saw an air of seriousness, which in reality dominated the man. When I returned to St. Louis on November 7, 1860, I wrote the following:

"Abraham Lincoln has been pictured to the world by his political and personal enemies as a jester, a comic story-teller, a common sort of jury lawyer whose special vocation it is to raise a laugh. But he is quite as serious as a majority of men and has a serious air at times which almost borders on the solemn. I believe he will be found serious enough when the occasion requires it, and that he may be depended upon to carry the people safely through the trying scenes to come." I recall these words now with some pleasure because they have been abundantly justified by later events.

"If the floor had opened and dropped me out of sight, I should have been happy"

The visitors in this account also misjudge Lincoln's serious-
ness, asking him to "tell us one of your good stories." The au-
thor, Colonel Silas W. Burt, is mortified.

AT THE instance of the Major, we made two attempts to
see the President at the White House, but were told that
he was too closely engaged to see anyone. Colonel Van
Buren and I appreciated the awful burden the great
leader was then bearing, and felt that we could not insist
upon an audience. The Major was enraged by what he assumed was an indignity to his cousin [Governor Seymour
of New York]. He was a type of one class of regular army
officers of the old days, brusque, with many oaths and a
taste for strong drink.

On the evening of Friday, June 26 [1863], Colonel Van
Buren, his son, then on a visit to Washington, and I were
occupying chairs on the sidewalk in front of Wormley's
Hotel, when the Major, arrayed in full uniform, drove up
in a hack, exclaiming: "Put on your toggery," meaning our
dress uniforms; "we are going to see Old Abe."

We asked for explanations, since we knew the President

[From Silas W. Burt, "Lincoln on His Own Storytelling," *Century* magazine,
February 1907]

spent his nights at a cottage on the beautiful grounds of
the Soldiers' Home, about two miles north of the city, and
it seemed the height of impertinence to pursue the fagged
official to his chosen retreat. Had we known then, as we
did later, that it was the evening of the day when he had
resolved upon that desperate military expedient, the
change of the commander of an army almost upon the eve
of a momentous conflict, we should have refused to go.
The Major said: "Horatio wrote me that you were to have
an interview with the President, and— —, you are bound
to have one!" His persistence finally overcame our
protests, and we hastened to put on our uniforms and to
start, young (John D.) Van Buren accompanying us.

It was a bright night and about nine o'clock when we
turned from the highway into the winding roads of the
Soldiers' Home. We saw gleaming amid the shrubbery in
all directions the bayonets of the soldiers who guarded the
President's residence. There were at that time many fears
expressed that a cavalry raid would be made for the purpose of capturing the President.

We drew up in front of a cottage before which a sentry
was walking to and fro. To him the Major gave some pass-
word, and we alighted with renewed trepidation, for the
aspect of the house indicated retirement for the night. The
Major rang the bell, and after a while the door was opened
by a man-servant, whom the Major peremptorily directed
to inform the President that some gentlemen, specially
empowered by Governor Seymour of New York, desired to
see him. The servant hesitated, but the Major's manner
was so urgent that we were admitted to a dimly lighted
hall, and ushered thence into a dark parlor, where the servant lighted a chandelier and departed with our cards.

During our drive, Colonel Van Buren and I had recognized the fact that the indomitable Major had primed himself thoroughly with his favorite whisky, as evidenced by his constant stroking of his heavy beard, a trick that denoted alcoholic repletion.

After the servant returned and announced that the President would receive us, we sat for some time in painful silence. At length we heard slow, shuffling steps come down the carpeted stairs, and the President entered the room as we respectfully rose from our seats. That pathetic figure has ever remained indelible in my memory. His tall form was bowed, his hair disheveled; he wore no necktie or collar, and his large feet were partly incased in very loose, heelless slippers. It was very evident that he had got up from his bed or had been very nearly ready to get into it when we were announced, and had hastily put on some clothing and those slippers that made the flip-flap sounds on the stairs.

It was the face that, in every line, told the story of anxiety and weariness. The drooping eyelids, looking almost swollen; the dark bags beneath the eyes; the deep marks about the large and expressive mouth; the flaccid muscles of the jaws, were all so majestically pitiful that I could almost have fallen on my knees and begged pardon for my part in the cruel presumption and impudence that had thus invaded his repose. As we were severally introduced, the President shook hands with us, and then took his seat on a haircloth-covered sofa beside the Major, while we others sat on chairs in front of him. Colonel Van Buren, in fitting words, conveyed the message from Governor Seymour, asking the President in Governor Seymour's name, to pay no attention to newspaper statements as to the governor's unfriendliness, and assured the President of the Governor's fixed intention to fulfill any constitutional call upon him for funds to support the Government. The President replied that he had attached no importance to the rumors referred to, and that he needed no formal assurances that the Governor would do all in his power to aid him.

The merely formal talk being over, something was said about the critical condition of military matters, and the President observed that he had no fears about the safety of Washington, and was certain that the attempted invasion of the Northern States would be arrested. He said the latest intelligence from the Army of the Potomac was favorable, but gave no details, and it was not until the next day that we learned that General Meade had succeeded General Hooker.

A little pause in the conversation ensued. The gaunt figure of the President had gradually slid lower on the slippery sofa, and his long legs were stretched out in front, the loose slippers half-fallen from his feet, while the drowsy eyelids had almost closed over his eyes, and his jaded features had taken on the suggestion of relaxation in sleep. I repeat that I never think of this noble man's personality without recalling him at that moment of supreme danger to the Republic and without seeing again that sad, worn countenance of the man who bore with such courage and patience his heavy burdens.

Deeply moved by the President's evident fatigue, and by his cordial treatment of us in spite of our presumptuous call, Colonel Van Buren and I were about rising to make our adieus when, to our dismay, the Major slapped the President on his knee and said: "Mr. President, tell us one of your good stories."

If the floor had opened and dropped me out of sight, I should have been happy.

The President drew himself up, and turning his back as far as possible upon the Major, with great dignity addressed the rest of us, saying: "I believe I have the popular reputation of being a story-teller, but I do not deserve the name in its general sense; for it is not the story itself, but its purpose, or effect, that interests me. I often avoid a long and useless discussion by others or a laborious explanation on my own part by a short story that illustrates my point of view. So, too, the sharpness of a refusal or the edge of a rebuke may be blunted by an appropriate story, so as to save wounded feeling and yet serve the purpose. No, I am not simply a story-teller, but story-telling as an emollient saves me much friction and distress." These are almost his exact words, of which I made a record that very night.

When the President had finished, we arose and made our salutations, and withdrew, our last view of our great leader being a countenance gracious, but inexpressibly sad.

I have told this adventure to many friends, some of whom have asked why I did not publish it. For many years I was loth to make a public statement of even unconsenting presence at such treatment of one whom the nation recognizes as ranking as high as Washington in our political history and venerates as a martyr. But I have been persuaded that this explanation by our beloved President of the great solace he derived from his story-telling should now be generally known.

"A simple grandeur and profound dignity"

Robert Brewster Stanton saw Lincoln many times while he visited the President with his father, the Reverend Robert Livingston Stanton. The young Stanton meets a very different president than the dames of Washington society had led him to believe.

IT HAS always been my belief that the reason why Abraham Lincoln and my father became such warm friends was because he brought to the President a certain inside knowledge of the South and its people, from an earnest and loyal follower, and Mr. Lincoln welcomed such direct information when they discussed together the perplexing problems of those days, as they so often did.

Thus it came about that I, even so young, going with my father, came to know Mr. Lincoln personally, and was able to sit with him for hours at a time, in his private office at the White House, and listen to those talks and discussions and observe him at close range, and study his every word and action at times when there was nothing to disturb, and when only one or two others were in the room.

. . . My father took me to see the President when he called to discuss with him some of those problems of the

[From Robert Brewster Stanton, "The Lincoln a Boy Saw and Knew," *Century* magazine, February 1920]

country and the war. My father was his personal friend and I did not wonder at his reception. But is it possible that I ever can forget the way Abraham Lincoln received me—a mere lad? His cordial manner, the warm grasp of that large, kind, gentle hand, the fascinating though almost evasive smile, and the simple word or two of welcome, were so earnest and sincere that I thought he intended me to understand—and so I felt—that he received me not as a boy, but as a man, though very young. That first warm hand-clasp (though later I had many more) from that good and great man is one of the most cherished memories of my life.

Through the whole of the campaign of 1860, while recognizing his ability, he had been characterized as Old Abe, the long, lank, gawky rail-splitter. On coming to Washington he had been ridiculed for the manner in which he had entered the city, and spoken of as that rough, uncouth Westerner from the prairies of Illinois who had dared to come among the exclusive, high-born, generally Southern people of the capital. I, as a boy, knew many of the families of those old, exclusive, pre-war Washingtonians, for I had lived there with my grandmother on my mother's side, an English woman who went to Washington about 1800, and I had heard, more particularly from the dames of society, those bitter, cutting remarks about Mr. Lincoln's uncouth mannerisms and uncivilized behavior.

What was my surprise, then, when I saw him and heard him at that first inauguration! There I saw a tall, square-shouldered man with long arms and legs, but, as he came down the east steps of the Capitol and onto the platform from which he spoke, he walked with such a dignified carriage and seeming perfect ease, that there was dispelled forever from my mind the idea that he was in any way un-

couth or at a loss to know the proper thing to do or how to
do it.

When he began to speak I was again surprised, on account of what I heard of him. He spoke so naturally, without any attempted oratorical effect, but with such an
earnest simplicity and firmness, that he seemed to me to
have but one desire as shown in his manner of speaking—
to draw that crowd close to him and talk to them as man
to man.

His manner was that of perfect self-possession. He
seemed to me to fully appreciate his new and unexpected
surroundings, to understand perfectly the enormous responsibilities he was undertaking, but at the same time to
have perfect confidence in himself that, with God's help,
which he always invoked, he could and would carry them
through to a successful conclusion. . . .

It is true that his figure was tall, lean, possibly lank, and
in a sense "ungainly." Yet with all this he had that dignity
of bearing, that purposeful, self-possessed, and natural
poise which, to me, not only demanded admiration but in-
spired reverence on almost every occasion.

. . . At one time I saw him under circumstances which,
if any could bring out those reputed defects in his carriage,
should have done so. It was at a meeting of the Houses of
Congress, gathered in the Hall of Representatives to cele-
brate some victory of the war. The chamber was packed,
and the galleries overflowed with men and women. I sat in
a front-row seat. The door opened on the opposite side,
and as the Marine Band played "Hail to the Chief," Mr.
Lincoln entered. The whole audience rose and cheered. He
glanced up at the throng and there appeared on his countenance a bright, beautiful, but gentle smile of thanks,
nothing more. In a moment this was gone, and holding

himself perfectly erect, with an expression of unconcern and self-possession, he walked across the hall up to the speaker's desk with a simple grandeur and profound dignity that would be difficult for anyone to surpass.

At another time I saw what at first surprised me greatly. It was at a great review of General McClellan's Army of the Potomac, that army that had been getting ready so long. Seventy-five thousand men of all arms were gathered on the Virginia plain, and a throng had come out from the capital to see them. In a little carriage my father, mother and I were among the spectators. We were placed within twenty feet of where the President's carriage stood. The military spectacle was of course inspiring, but what interested me more was observing Mr. Lincoln's part in the grand review.

Only lately I was asked, here in New York, whether it was true that Mr. Lincoln went to that review dressed in an old, yellowish linen suit. It was not. He was dressed in his accustomed black broadcloth, long frock coat, and usual high silk hat, this time a new one.

I was close enough to him to clearly note his every movement and see the expression of his face. As the commander-in-chief of the army and navy of the United States rode down that long line, mounted on a magnificent charger, followed by the general and his staff, he sat and rode his horse as if it were the one thing in the world he knew how to do. He sat perfectly erect, not stiffly, but at perfect ease, and in all that throng of trained military men there was not a general who bore himself with . . . as much dignity, and rode with more true military bearing than the President.

This was one time when I saw him, as he rode down the line, when his face seemed never to change. His eyes then were not listless, his whole countenance beamed with one expression—that of pride in the thoroughly organized army that he believed would bring victory.

Part Two

LINCOLN IN CARPET SLIPPERS

AFTER waiting patiently, it is finally your turn to speak
with the president. As you approach, Lincoln rises from
his chair and shakes your hand, asking you cordially what
he can do for you. As you begin speaking, you both sit
down. He leans forward, clasps his knee with both hands,
and gazes at you with a serious, intent expression. His features seem somewhat dull and lifeless, but as you are talking you remind him of something that amuses him or
interests him. His expression changes. His face lights up,
the melancholy eyes come alive with enthusiasm and interest. You are struck by his simplicity, his artlessness, his
lack of pretense. He seems genuinely interested in what
you are saying. You can tell from his hair and his lack of a
good tailor that he is genuinely uninterested in the impression he is making. You are drawn to him feeling that
he understands you, does not think less of you than he
does of himself, that he takes his position to be one perhaps of higher authority but not superiority. You continue
to tell your story as you would to a good friend or kindly
neighbor, surprised that you do not feel intimidated talking to the President of the United States.

"His simplicity and artlessness"

Noah Brooks, a journalist, was one of Lincoln's closest friends. Brooks sums up Lincoln's humility and lack of pretentiousness this way.

ALL PERSONS agree that the most marked characteristic of Mr. Lincoln's manners was his simplicity and artlessness; this immediately impressed itself upon the observation of those who met him for the first time, and each successive interview deepened the impression. People seemed delighted to find in the ruler of the nation freedom from pomposity and affectation, mingled with a certain simple dignity which never forsook him. Though oppressed with the weight of responsibility resting upon him as President of the United States, he shrank from assuming any of the honors, or even the titles, of the position. After years of intimate acquaintance with Mr. Lincoln the writer can not now recall a single instance in which he spoke of himself as President, or used that title for himself, except when acting in an official capacity. He always spoke of his position and office vaguely, as "this place," "here," or other modest phrase. Once, speaking of the room in the Capitol used by the President of the United

[From Noah Brooks, "Personal Recollections of Abraham Lincoln," *Harper's Monthly*, May 1865]

States during the close of a session of Congress, he said, "That room, you know, that they call"—dropping his voice and hesitating—"the President's room." To an intimate friend who addressed him always by his own proper title he said, "Now call me Lincoln, and I'll promise not to tell of the breach of etiquette—if you won't—and I shall have a resting-spell from 'Mr. President.'"

"[A] frank, bland and familiar manner"

Reverend Cornelius van Santwood, who was at the White House on one of Lincoln's "public days," tells of the president's typical reception of visitors.

A WHITE-HAIRED, gentlemanly-looking person, in company with his daughter, who seemed quite young and was certainly very pretty and prepossessing, though she had a shy, bashful, and even frightened look, met with a most courteous and friendly reception. The gentleman said he had no business to transact and would not trespass on the President's time, that he had come simply to see and salute him, and to present his daughter, who had longed to have this honor before returning to their distant home. Mr. Lincoln greeted them very cordially, rising and shaking hands with them, and with the frank, bland and familiar manner which made strangers feel unconstrained and at ease in his presence, he chatted pleasantly, even playfully, with them for some minutes, to the evident delight of both visitors. When they were about to go away, he politely escorted them to a door opening into the hall, and different from that through which the visitors entered, and dismissed them with charming courtesy.

[From Cornelius van Santwood, "A Reception by President Lincoln," *Century* magazine, April 1883]

"All my uneasiness and awe vanished in a moment before the homely greeting of the President"

George Borrett, an English barrister visiting America, went to see Lincoln late at night at the cottage at the Soldiers' Home (the Lincolns' summer residence not far from the White House) with a Miss Harrington, the daughter of George Harrington, assistant secretary of the treasury. Although the Lincolns' servant suggested it was "rather late" for an interview, Miss Harrington insisted, and the visitors were ushered into "a moderate-sized, neatly furnished drawing room, where [they] were told the President would see [them] immediately." Borrett wrote home about the evening.

WE HAD SAT there but a few minutes, when there entered through the folding doors the long, lanky, lath-like figure (of the President) . . . with hair ruffled, and eyes very sleepy, and—hear it, ye votaries of court etiquette! — feet enveloped in carpet slippers. We all rose somewhat confused by this abrupt introduction to the presence of the highest in the land, except, of course, the Secretary's daughter, who immediately offered her hand to the President, and in a few apt words explained who she was, and

[From George Borrett, *Letters from Canada and the United States*, London, 1865]

why she was there. Mr. Lincoln advanced to me and my fellow-travellers, shook each of us warmly by the hand, expressed his pleasure at seeing us, and told us to take seats and make ourselves comfortable. We did so, and were at home at once. All my uneasiness and awe vanished in a moment before the homely greeting of the President, and the genial smile which accompanied it; and had they not, a glance at one of the carpet slippers jogging up and down upon the knee of the other leg in the most delightful freedom of attitude, would have reassured me. . . .

The conversation was briskly kept up by the President. It began, naturally enough, with questions about our tour, and the invariable interrogation that every American puts to a stranger as to what he thinks of "our great country"; and then, after a passing allusion to the war, and a remark that we were seeing his country at an unfortunate time, Mr. Lincoln turned to England, and its political aspect and constitution; and thence he went off, unasked, into a forcibly drawn sketch of the constitution of the United States, and the material points of difference between the governments of the two countries. . . . We had heard several (expositions on the American Constitution) before this, and began to get rather tired of them; but we were glad, of course, to listen to anything upon the matter from the highest authority in the land, especially as his commentary was very lucid and intelligent. Of course he asked what our trade was; and hearing that it was law, he launched off into some shrewd remarks about the legal systems of the two countries. . . .

The conversation next turned upon English poetry, the president saying that when we disturbed him he was deep in Pope. He seemed to be a great admirer of Pope, especially of his "Essay on Man"; going so far as to say that he thought it contained all the religious instruction which it was necessary for a man to know. Then he mused for a moment or two, and asked us if we could show him any finer lines than those ending, as he quoted them without hesitation—

"All nature is but art, unknown to thee;
All chance, direction, which thou canst not see;
All discord, harmony not understood;
All partial evil, universal good;
And, spite of pride, in erring treason's spite,
One truth is clear, whatever is, is right."

And here, on getting to the last few words, his instinctive humor broke out, for to an extremely flat remark of mine upon the beauty of the verses he had repeated, he replied with a smile—

"Yes, that's a convenient line, too, the last one. You see, a man may turn it, and say, 'Well, if whatever *is* is right, why, then, whatever *isn't* must be wrong.'"

And then he went off into a broad laugh, and we laughed, too—not so much at the joke, which we thought decidedly poor, as at the way in which he delivered himself of it. The laugh ended, and I rose to go. I had heard the President make a joke—a very mild one, it is true—but I felt that the second great object of my visit to the country (Niagara being my first) had been achieved. . . . The Secretary's daughter, after . . . (a) hint at her regret that we could not have the chance of seeing Mrs. Lincoln—to which the President replied, "I guess we shall not get to see Mrs. Lincoln down here again tonight"—arose and thanked him for his courtesy in according us so pleasant an interview; and the President, in return, assured her and us that the meeting had been equally agreeable to himself;

and thanking us cordially for coming to see him, gave us each a hearty grip of the hand—it was much more than a shake—and we withdrew.

The Soldiers' Home, where the Lincolns often spent the summer

"A game of romps"

Francis B. Carpenter, who stayed at the White House while working on a portrait of the president, had the opportunity to observe Lincoln on a daily basis. He published his impressions in a book, Six Months at the White House, *from which this excerpt is taken. In this account Carpenter quotes the Honorable W. D. Kelly, who offered the following characterization of Lincoln in an address he gave in Philadelphia after Lincoln's death.*

"PRESIDENT Lincoln," says the Hon. W. D. Kelly, "was a large and many-sided man, and yet so simple that no one, not even a child, could approach him without feeling that he had found in him a sympathizing friend. I remember that I apprised him of the fact that a lad, the son of one of my townsmen, had served a year on board the gunboat *Ottawa*, and had been in two important engagements; in the first as a powder-monkey, when he had conducted himself with such coolness that he had been chosen as captain's messenger in the second; and I suggested to the President that it was in his power to send to the Naval School, annually, three boys who had served at least a year in the navy."

[From Francis B. Carpenter, *Six Months at the White House with Abraham Lincoln*, New York, 1866]

"He at once wrote on the back of a letter from the commander of the *Ottawa*, which I had handed him, to the Secretary of the Navy: 'If the appointments for this year have not been made, let this boy be appointed.' The appointment had not been made, and I brought it home with me. It directed the lad to report for examination at the school in July. Just as he was ready to start, his father, looking over the law, discovered that he could not report until he was fourteen years of age, which he would not be until September following. The poor child sat down and wept. He feared that he was not to go to the Naval School. He was, however, soon consoled by being told that 'the President could make it right.' It was my fortune to meet him the next morning at the door of the executive chamber with his father.

"Taking by the hand the little fellow,—short for his age, dressed in the sailor's blue pants and shirt,—I advanced with him to the President, who sat in his usual seat, and said: 'Mr. President, my young friend, Willie Bladen, finds a difficulty about his appointment. You have directed him to appear at the school in July; but he is not yet fourteen years of age.' But before I got half of this out, Mr. Lincoln, laying down his spectacles, rose and said: 'Bless me! is that the boy who did so gallantly in those two battles? Why, I feel that I should bow to him, and not he to me.'

"The little fellow had made his graceful bow. The president took the papers at once, and as soon as he learned that a postponement till September would suffice, made the order that the lad should report in that month. Then putting his hand on Willie's head, he said: 'Now, my boy, go home and have good fun during the two months, for they are about the last holiday you will get.' The little fellow bowed himself out, feeling that the President of the

United States, though a very great man, was one that he would nevertheless like to have a game of romps with."

Francis B. Carpenter, who painted the president's portrait

"There was safety in his atmosphere"

Frederick Douglass, the fiery abolitionist leader, met Lincoln several times. Although Douglass sometimes disagreed with Lincoln, he was greatly impressed with the way Lincoln received him, and with the ease he felt in Lincoln's presence.

I DO NOT know more about Mr. Lincoln than is known by countless thousands of Americans who have met the man. But I am quite willing to give my recollections of him and the impressions made by him upon my mind as to his character.

My first interview with him was in the summer of 1863, soon after the Confederate States had declared their purpose to treat colored soldiers as insurgents, and their purpose not to treat any such soldiers as prisoners of war subject to exchange like other soldiers. My visit to Mr. Lincoln was in reference to this threat of the Confederate States. I was at the time engaged in raising colored troops, and I desired some assurances from President Lincoln that such troops should be treated as soldiers of the United States, and when taken prisoners exchanged like other soldiers; that when any of them were hanged or enslaved the President should retaliate. I was introduced to

[From Allen Thorndike Rice, ed., *Reminiscences of Abraham Lincoln by Distinguished Men of His Time*, New York, 1886]

Mr. Lincoln by Senator Pomeroy, of Kansas; I met him at the Executive Mansion.

I was somewhat troubled with the thought of meeting one so august and high in authority, especially as I had never been in the White House before and had never spoken to a President of the United States before. But my embarrassment soon vanished when I met the face of Mr. Lincoln. When I entered he was seated in a low chair, surrounded by a multitude of books and papers, his feet and legs were extended in front of his chair. On my approach he slowly drew his feet in from the different parts of the room into which they had strayed, and he began to rise, and continued to rise until he looked down upon me, and extended his hand and gave me a welcome. I began, with some hesitation, to tell him who I was and what I had been doing, but he soon stopped me, saying in a sharp, cordial voice: "You need not tell me who you are, Mr. Douglass, I know who you are, Mr. Sewell has told me all about you." He then invited me to take a seat beside him. Not wishing to occupy his time and attention, seeing that he was busy, I stated to him the object of my call at once. I said, "Mr. Lincoln I am recruiting colored troops. I have assisted in fitting up two regiments in Massachusetts, and am now at work in the same way in Pennsylvania, and have come to say this to you, sir, if you wish to make this branch of the service successful you must do four things.

"First, you must give colored soldiers the same pay that you give white soldiers.

"Second, you must compel the Confederate States to treat colored soldiers, when taken prisoners, as prisoners of war.

"Third, when any colored man or soldier performs brave meritorious exploits in the field, you must enable me to say to those that I recruit that they will be promoted for such service, precisely as white men are promoted for similar service.

"Fourth, in case any colored soldiers are murdered in cold blood and taken prisoners you should retaliate in kind."

To this little speech Mr. Lincoln listened with earnest attention and with very apparent sympathy, and replied to each point in his own peculiar forcible way. First he spoke of the opposition generally to employing negroes as soldiers at all, of the prejudice against the race, and of the advantage to colored people that would result from their being employed as soldiers in defence of their country. He regarded such an employment as an experiment, and spoke of the advantage it would be to the colored race if the experiment should succeed. He said that he had difficulty in getting colored men into the United States uniform; that when the purpose was fixed to employ them as soldiers, several different uniforms were proposed for them, and that it was something gained when it was finally determined to clothe them like other soldiers.

Now, as to the pay, we had to make some concession to prejudice. There were threats that if we made soldiers of them at all white men would not enlist, would not fight beside them. Besides, it was not believed that a negro could make a good soldier, as good a soldier as a white man, and hence it was thought that he should not have the same pay as a white man. But said he, "I assure you, Mr. Douglass, that in the end they shall have the same pay as white soldiers." As to the exchange and general treatment of soldiers when taken prisoners of war, he should insist to their being entitled to all privileges of such prisoners. Mr. Lincoln admitted the justice of my demand for the promotion of colored soldiers for good conduct in the field, but on the matter of retaliation he differed from me entirely. I shall never forget the benignant expression of his face, the tearful look of his eye and the quiver of his voice, when he deprecated a resort to retaliatory measures. "Once begun," said he, "I do not know where such a measure would stop." He said he could not take men out and kill them in cold blood for what was done by others. If he could get hold of the persons who were guilty of killing the colored prisoners in cold blood, the case would be different, but he could not kill the innocent for the guilty.

Before leaving Mr. Lincoln, Senator Pomeroy said:

"Mr. President, Mr. Stanton is going to make Douglass Adjutant-General to General Thomas, and is going to send him down the Mississippi to recruit."

Mr. Lincoln said in answer to this: "I will sign any commission that Mr. Stanton will give Mr. Douglass." At this we parted.

I met Mr. Lincoln several times after this interview.

. . . I was present at the inauguration of Mr. Lincoln, the 4th of March, 1865. I felt then that there was murder in the air, and I kept close to his carriage on the way to the Capitol, for I felt that I might see him fall that day. It was a vague presentiment.

At that time the Confederate cause was on its last legs, as it were, and there was deep feeling. I could feel it in the atmosphere here. I did not know exactly what it was, but I just felt as if he might be shot on his way to the Capitol. I cannot refer to any incident, in fact, to any expression that I heard, it was simply a presentiment that Lincoln might fall that day. I got right in front of the east portico of the Capitol, listened to his inaugural address, and witnessed his being sworn in by Chief Justice Chase. When he came on the steps he was accompanied by Vice-President Johnson. In looking out in the crowd he saw me standing near by, and I could see he was pointing me out to Andrew Johnson. Mr. Johnson, without knowing perhaps that I saw the movement, looked quite annoyed that his attention should be called in that direction. So I got a peep into his soul. As soon as he saw me looking at him, suddenly he assumed rather an amicable expression of countenance. I felt that, whatever else the man might be, he was no friend to my people.

I heard Mr. Lincoln deliver this wonderful address. It was very short; but he answered all the objections raised to his prolonging the war in one sentence—it was a remarkable sentence.

"Fondly do we hope, profoundly do we pray, that this mighty scourge of war shall soon pass away, yet if God wills it continue until all the wealth piled up by two hundred years of bondage shall have been wasted, and each drop of blood drawn by the lash shall have been paid for by one drawn by the sword, we must still say, as was said three thousand years ago, the judgments of the Lord are true and righteous altogether."

For the first time in my life, and I suppose the first time in any colored man's life, I attended the reception of President Lincoln on the evening of the inauguration. As I approached the door I was seized by two policemen and forbidden to enter. I said to them that they were mistaken entirely in what they were doing, that if Mr. Lincoln knew that I was at the door he would order my admission, and I bolted in by them. On the inside I was taken charge of by two other policemen, to be conducted as I supposed to the President, but instead of that they were conducting me out the window on a plank.

"Oh," said I, "this will not do, gentlemen," and as a gentleman was passing in I said to him, "Just say to Mr. Lincoln that Fred. Douglass is at the door."

He rushed in to President Lincoln, and almost in less than a half a minute I was invited into the East Room of the White House. A perfect sea of beauty and elegance, too, it was. The ladies were in very fine attire, and Mrs. Lincoln was standing there. I could not have been more than ten feet from him when Mr. Lincoln saw me; his countenance lighted up, and he said in a voice which was heard all around: "Here comes my friend Douglass." As I approached him he reached out his hand, gave me a cordial shake, and said: "Douglass, I saw you in the crowd today listening to my inaugural address. There is no man's opinion that I value more than yours: what do you think of it?" I said: "Mr. Lincoln, I cannot stop here to talk with you, as there are thousands waiting to shake you by the hand"; but he said again: "What did you think of it?" I said: "Mr. Lincoln, it was a sacred effort," and then I walked off. "I am glad you liked it," he said. That was the last time I saw him to speak with him.

In all my interviews with Mr. Lincoln I was impressed with his entire freedom from popular prejudice against the colored race. He was the first great man that I talked with in the United States freely, who in no single instance reminded me of the difference between himself and myself, of the difference of color, and I thought that all the more remarkable because he came from a state where there were black laws. I account partially for his kindness to me because of the similarity with which I had fought my way up, we both starting at the lowest round of the ladder. . . .

Then, too, there was another feeling that I had with reference to him, and that was that while I felt I was in the presence of a very great man, as great as the greatest, I felt as though I could go and put my hand on him if I wanted to, to put my hand on his shoulder. Of course I did not do it, but I felt that I could. I felt as though I was in the presence of a big brother, and that there was safety in his atmosphere.

Frederick Douglass

"The closer I approached the great man . . . the less I feared him"

In this account, John M. Bullock goes to see President Lincoln to seek the parole of his brother, Lieutenant Waller R. Bullock, a Confederate officer who is sick and wounded. John Bullock wishes his brother paroled so he can be brought home to die.

. . . LEARNING that Mr. Lincoln was that morning holding a levee at the White House, I took my leave of the Postmaster General, after thanking him for all he had done for me, and strolled over in that direction. I had never before been present at a Presidential reception, and the sight was indeed a novel one.

Mr. Lincoln was standing in the center of one of the small rooms—the Blue Room, I believe; and near him, and a little in his rear, were Mrs. Lincoln and some half-dozen ladies, wives of members of the cabinet. In animated conversation with Mrs. Lincoln and her guests were a number of officers of the army and navy, several generals and admirals among them. The President stood alone. There were no introductions. Each person came up and shook his hand, and passed on to give place to those that

[From John M. Bullock, "President Lincoln's Visiting Card," *Century* magazine, February 1889]

followed. During this ceremony the Marine Band, stationed in the East Room, played for the marching throng. I had noticed one thing of which I had determined to take advantage. In the interval between the time the band ceased to play one selection and the beginning of another piece, the people stopped passing through the Blue Room, and for the time being left the President entirely alone. He stood with his hands clasped in front of him, his head slightly bowed, in his eyes that far-away look so often spoken of by those who knew him well. I thought this a splendid opportunity to get speech of him. Had I been older, I should not have thrust myself upon him at such a time; but youth does not stop to enquire too closely into the courtesies of life. Just as the band ceased playing, I stepped up to Mr. Lincoln, shook him by the hand, and said: "Mr. President, I am a son of the Rev. Dr. Bullock of Baltimore, whom you know; and I have come to ask that you will parole my brother, Walter R. Bullock, who is a Confederate lieutenant, now in prison at Johnson's Island, wounded and sick." I of course supposed Mr. Lincoln would reply to my petition by granting it or dismissing me with a refusal. But ignoring what I had said altogether, he asked in quite a loud voice—enough so to attract the notice of all those about him: "You are a nephew of John C. Breckinridge, ain't you?" "Yes, sir," I replied. "Then I suppose, when you are old enough, you will be going down to fight us," said Mr. Lincoln, in rather a laughing tone. "Yes, sir," I replied; "I suppose, when I am old enough, I will join the army." Mr. Lincoln seemed to be somewhat amused at my answer, and placing his hand upon my shoulder, said in a kind, fatherly way: "My son, you come back here at four o'clock this afternoon, and I will see you then." I could see, from the cessation of all conversation by the persons about the President, including both Mrs. Lincoln and her guest, that they were interested listeners to our interview.

As the first person came up to take Mr. Lincoln's hand after the band began to play once more, I retired, bowing myself out, only too well pleased to have an engagement with so important a person as the President of the United States, the man who held the life of my brother in his keeping. Thinking I would speak to the doorkeeper at the main entrance of the mansion as to my prospects of gaining admittance to Mr. Lincoln's presence, at four o'clock, I asked that official how it would be, telling him what the President has said. "He just said that to keep from hurting your feelings, young fellow; for I have positive orders from Mr. Lincoln in person to close these doors at two o'clock sharp, and not allow anybody to come in—not even members of the cabinet." I had more confidence in Mr. Lincoln's word than the doorkeeper of the White House, and went my way without fear and full of hope. After satisfying a growing boy's appetite at Willard's Hotel,—a matter of time,—I counted the minutes until the hour named.

As I approached the White House, to my surprise and gratification I saw Mr. Lincoln standing upon the west end of the front portico, with his son Robert by his side. Robert, then a lad, had lately been appointed Assistant Adjutant-General and assigned to duty with General Grant; and he and his father, I discovered, were negotiating for the purchase of a horse suitable for service in the field. As I stepped up and took a position near the President, an orderly was in the act of riding a stylish-looking animal up and down one of the driveways in front of the mansion. I stood silently by, listening to the comments of the quiet, businesslike father and the more enthusiastic son, until suddenly Mr. Lincoln turned to where I stood, and said: "My son, you are a Kentuckian, and ought to know something about the value of horses. Tell me, what do you think that one is worth?" pointing to the animal in question. I replied, "I should like to see how he is gaited, sir, before I decide." "Ride that horse around a little more," called the President to the orderly, "and let us see how he goes." After looking him over for a few minutes, and noticing the fact that he was a fairly good saddle-horse, I gave my opinion that he was worth about one hundred and fifty dollars. My decision seemed to have co-incided with that of Mr. Lincoln; for he said in a rather loud voice, easily heard by the rider, who had topped his horse near the end of the portico: "Just what I said he was worth—just what I offered him; but he wanted two hundred dollars for him—more than I thought he was worth." In a few moments, however, the sale was made at the President's figure; and seemingly much to Robert's delight, the horse was ordered to be delivered to the White House stables. Upon the conclusion of the purchase, Mr. Lincoln walked slowly to the main entrance and passed in, saying to me as he did so, "Follow me, my son." Very deliberately Mr. Lincoln mounted the stairway, and as he gained the hallway above looked around to see if I had accompanied him. Then opening a door to his right, he went into an office where was seated John Hay, secretary to Mr. Lincoln, before a large open fire, writing busily. Mr. Lincoln said, "Take a seat, my son; I will be back in a few moments"; and picking up a small package of mail from the desk near him, opened a door to the adjoining office and went out, leaving me to the companionship of Mr. Hay, who soon retired as if on important business.

I occupied myself during Mr. Lincoln's brief absence in trying to collect my thoughts and prepare a set speech to pour into his sympathetic ears. Suddenly the door opened, and the tall form of the President, six feet four inches in height, towered above me. Closing the door quietly behind him, he drew the largest of the easy-chairs to one side of the glowing log fire, and sitting down, leaned his elbow on the arm toward me, and said, "Now, my son, what can I do for you?" You will note that all through my interviews with Mr. Lincoln he never addressed me without using the words—very kindly they sounded, too—"my son." Where now was my set speech? That I never knew. All I saw before me was a kind, sorrowful face, ready to listen to my story. I was not in the least embarrassed, as I supposed I should be, and at once began to tell Mr. Lincoln what I had come to ask of him. I said: "Mr. President, I have come to ask you to parole my brother, Lieutenant Waller R. Bullock, from Johnson's Island, where he is sick and wounded. He is extremely ill, and I want you to release him so that he may be brought home to die." I knew what he would ask me the first thing, and my heart sank as I heard the fateful question put. "Will your brother take the oath [of allegiance to the Union]?" said Mr. Lincoln. "No, sir; he will not," I replied. "He will have to die in prison if that is the only alternative." "I cannot parole him," said the President. "I should like to do so; but it is impossible unless he will take the oath." I replied: "Mr. Lincoln, my brother is very ill, and cannot live long in his present condition; and it would be a great comfort to our invalid mother to have him brought home so that he can be tenderly nursed until he dies." "My son," said Mr. Lincoln, "I should like to grant your request, but I cannot do it. You don't know what a pressure is brought to bear upon me in such matters. Why, there are senators and members of congress that would be glad to have their relatives and friends paroled on such terms as you ask, and cannot accomplish it." Though somewhat disheartened, I again repeated the story of my brother's extreme illness, and the comfort it would be to my mother to have him with her in his dying condition. I said: "Mr. Lincoln, this is a case of life and death. If my brother remains much longer in prison on that bleak, dreary island, exposed to all the severity of an exceptionally cold winter, he cannot last very much longer. You are the only person in the United States that can do absolutely as you please in such matters; and you can release him if you desire to do so, no matter what people say or think." Mr. Lincoln had so often said that it was impossible for him to parole Waller that I felt my last chance to gain his consent to my petition was to appeal to him as the court of last resort, and throw the consequences of refusal upon him personally. Finally Mr. Lincoln sank into a state of deep meditation. He sat with his elbows on his knees, his face in his hands, and gazed long and intently into the great wood fire. He was not a handsome man; neither was he a graceful one. His appearance when in repose was rather dull and listless. Indeed, I was struck with his awkwardness while receiving the guests at his levee, walking upstairs, and sitting in his chair. His hair was cut unevenly on the back of his head, his features were rugged, and he had evidently paid but little regard to his tailor. I noticed how large his hands and feet were, how loosely his black suit hung upon his immense frame. And then, too, as I have before remarked, he had that far-away look in his eyes so often spoken of by those who knew him intimately during those awful years of blood and carnage, when his great soul was wrung with the anguish of a nation at war with itself.

Suddenly, without warning, and when, from his long silence, I had concluded my cause was lost, Mr. Lincoln sprang to his feet, his whole being alert, his eyes no longer dull, but clear and strong with the light of intense feeling and power, all the awkwardness gone, his face not handsome, but full of strength and intelligence, making it a pleasant face to look upon—one a child would not refuse to caress. Straightening himself to his full height, he brought his clenched hand down upon the desk with a bang, and said, as he looked me full in the face, "I'll do it; I'll do it!" Walking over to his desk, he picked up a small paper card case which held visiting-cards such as ladies generally use. Mr. Lincoln held it between his first finger and thumb up to his ear, and shook it to see if there were any cards left. I could distinctly hear the rattle of a single card. Finding what he was looking for, the President sat down, and placing the card before him, wrote very slowly and deliberately. I supposed he was writing an order to some clerk, or to John Hay, to have the parole papers made out. Such was my ignorance of the forms necessary to liberate prisoners that I imagined I should see a large official document with signatures and counter-signatures, seals, etc. Therefore, I was much surprised when Mr. Lincoln arose, and, holding the card between his forefinger and thumb, read it aloud to me as follows:

Allow Lieut. Waller R. Bullock to be paroled and go to his parents in Baltimore, and remain there until well enough to be exchanged.

A. Lincoln

Mr. Lincoln then held out the card to me; and seeing that I was somewhat disappointed in the size of the document, and hesitated to accept it, he said, as a smile played about the corners of his mouth: "That'll fetch him; that'll fetch him." I thanked the President with all the warmth of my being. I felt that by the act of clemency he had just shown my brother had a chance for his life, and that it was to Mr. Lincoln's kindness of heart and love of humanity that I owed the success of my mission. After once more expressing my thanks to the President, and assuring him of the gratitude of my father and mother and of our entire family, I prepared to take my leave, filled with joy. After handing me the card, Mr. Lincoln drew up one of the easy-chairs before the fire, and throwing himself into a comfortable position, began to ask me several questions. Said he: "Do you ever hear from your uncle John C. Breckinridge?" "Yes, sir," I replied: "we hear once in a while from prisoners coming through on special exchange; and sometimes we have been enabled to receive letters via City Point by flag of truce." "Well," said Mr. Lincoln. "I was fond of John, and I was sorry to see him take the course he did. Yes, I was fond of John, and regret that he sided with the South. It was a mistake." And then he made some further remarks about my uncle which showed his kind feeling for him. He also referred to his visit to Kentucky soon after his marriage, and the pleasant recollection he had of that period. (He had spent a few weeks in Fayette County at my grandfather Bullock's, whose second wife was an aunt of Mrs. Lincoln.) Altogether he was very kind, and I left the White House with my heart overflowing with gratitude to the President. . . .

Much has been said and written in regard to Mr. Lincoln's character for kindness, his disposition to be merciful, his gentleness toward those in trouble, his leniency to those in distress, his clemency, and desire, when possible, to pardon those who were condemned to death. All this is no doubt true. The testimony of those who knew him best confirms all that can be said in his praise as to the noble nature of the man. I wish, however, to bear witness to one fact regarding Mr. Lincoln that impressed me, boy as I was, in a marked degree during my interviews with him. Before approaching the President I felt a natural diffidence, not to say awe, of the man who was Chief Executive of the nation, commander-in-chief of the army and navy, as well as the man who held the life of my brother in his keeping. To a boy of fifteen this feeling was only natural. The closer I approached the great man, however, the less I feared him, the higher my courage rose; and before the interview was over I was as much at my ease with President Lincoln as if talking to my own father. The reasons for this are to be found in just the qualities of heart with which he is accredited, and rightly so, by all the world. No sooner had he laid his hand upon my shoulder and said, "My son," that I felt drawn to him, and dreaded less and less the interview he had granted me; and each successive question he asked me put me more at my ease, until, when I was alone with him in his private office, all my embarrassment vanished, and I saw before me the countenance of a man I could trust, one which invited confidence. And thus it was that I saw this man at the head of a great nation engaged in the most stupendous war in the history of the world. All of his hours were spent in labor. His time was priceless. Senators, representatives in Congress, ambassadors of foreign courts, officers of the army and navy, were anxious and pressing for an interview, however brief: members of the cabinet were debarred, according to the testimony of the doorkeeper. And yet, at such a time, this man of the people, this man among men, with the burden of a nation at war upon his shoulders, his mind bowed down by such responsibilities as no man ever bore alone since the world began—not even Napoleon at the height of his fame,—left all these mighty questions and affairs of state long enough to enter into the pleasure of his soldier boy; long enough to give ear to the petition of a young lad praying for a brother's life—and that brother, in his eyes, an enemy of the state; long enough to leave his home to go and pay respect to a dying friend in his last hours. Such was Abraham Lincoln as I saw him in 1865.

Mr. Lincoln was slain by a madman. No section should be held responsible for such a deed. The South mourned as truly for his death as did the North. The assassination of Mr. Lincoln deprived that portion of our country of a protector both able and willing to stand their friend during all those days of struggling poverty and misery consequent of four years of war.

None more truly felt genuine sorrow for the death of Mr. Lincoln than my father and his family. To each one of us it came as a personal loss. And when, as one man, the nation bowed its head in the presence of death, and with mournful hearts and kindly hands draped its homes with the trappings of woe, no heart in all the land beat with truer sympathy, and no hands touched with greater reverence the funereal emblems that gave utterance to our respect for the nation's dead, than his to whom Abraham Lincoln had granted liberty and life.

Part Three

LINCOLN'S MERCY

MORE TIMES than you can remember you have heard
Lincoln blamed for the war. You have heard many people
say that Lincoln is callous, a coldhearted tyrant who
wants to crush the South at any cost. But when you first
mention the war you can see the sadness in Lincoln's eyes,
the hint of grief and affliction. As you go on, a faraway
look comes to Lincoln's eyes. He seems to be lost in
thought, his expression remarkably pensive, inexpressibly
pained, as if a reservoir of tears lies very near the surface.
After a while, by an effort of will, he shakes off this
weight, and his generous and open disposition reappears.
You talk to him about the South, but surprisingly he refuses to let you speak of them as the enemy. He says he
will not have anyone use that word. The South is mis-
guided, he says, but not the enemy. Finally you tell him
the exact reason you are there—to receive a pardon for a
relative accused of cowardice. More quickly than you expected, he writes out orders for the pardon you had desired. He tells you he is particularly sympathetic to those
accused of cowardice because he does not know how he
himself would react in battle. "I have not fully made up
my mind," he says, "how I should behave when mini-balls

were whistling, and those great oblong shells shrieking in my ear. I might run away."

"My heart is like lead"

Lincoln commiserates with a father who has lost a son at Gettysburg, in this account written by E. W. Andrews.

DURING the ride to Gettysburg the President placed every one who approached him at his ease, relating numerous stories, some of them laughable, and others of a character that deeply touched the hearts of his listeners.

I remember well his reply to a gentleman who stated that [his] only son fell on "Little Round Top" at Gettysburg, and [he was] going to look at the spot.

President Lincoln replied: "You have been called upon to make a terrible sacrifice for the Union, and a visit to that spot, I fear, will open your wounds afresh. But oh! my dear sir, if we had reached the end of such sacrifices, and had nothing left for us to do but to place garlands on the graves of those who have already fallen, we could give thanks even amidst our tears; but when I think of the sacrifices of life yet to be offered and the hearts and homes yet to be made desolate before this dreadful war, so wickedly forced upon us, is over, my heart is like lead within me, and I feel, at times, like hiding in deep darkness."

[From Allen Thorndike Rice, ed., *Reminiscences of Abraham Lincoln by Distinguished Men of His Time*, New York, 1886]

"May the whole terrible thing soon end"

These are the recollections of George D. Gitt, who met Lincoln when he came to Gettysburg to deliver his famous address. Even in their brief meeting, Gitt has a glimpse of the president's weariness and deep sadness over the war.

AS EVERY ONE knows, the simplicity, the quiet kindliness which were so much a part of the great Lincoln, became more than ever manifest when he spoke those few classic words that make up the Gettysburg Address. But the writhings of soul of the magnanimous Lincoln, as revealed at that moment when private anxieties as well as the grave national crisis wrung his heart almost to the breaking point, lie recorded only in the memories of those few of us still living who saw and heard him on that Day of the Dedication, as November 19, 1863, is still familiarly called in and around Gettysburg.

Threescore and ten years have passed away since that address fell upon the ears of an assemblage that stood, as I well remember, motionless and silent. Many bowed their heads and, almost without exception, men doffed their hats. They mistook the speech for a prayer. A group of Negroes moaned forth an "Amen" in each pause.

[From George D. Gitt, "First Meetings with Lincoln in War Days," *Liberty* magazine, November 1933]

I, a boy of fifteen, intent upon being as close to Lincoln as was physically possible without being on top of the platform, had concealed myself earlier in the day among the huge store boxes that formed the foundations of the structure; and, during the delivery of the address I stood with my heart in my mouth, literally at the feet of my hero. Early in the evening of the previous day I had heard the shrill whistling of a locomotive at an hour when no train ever entered our village of Hanover, which lies about fourteen miles east of Gettysburg and a mile or two farther north of the Mason-Dixon line. Immediately I hastened toward the station, but not alone, for others had heard the whistling and were equally curious.

To my vast surprise I discovered that the special train on which Lincoln was journeying to Gettysburg had developed a hot box, and was therefore being shunted from the main line into the Hanover siding. Of course some had assumed that there would be no stop after a junction point ten miles to the east, and consequently, earlier in the day had gone there, hoping to get a glimpse of the President. But enough townsmen had remained at home so that within a few minutes after the first whistle blasts a crowd surrounded the coach in which Lincoln sat writing the latter part of his address, the top of his high hat serving as a makeshift desk.

There was no cheering. The babble of the crowd was subdued. The locomotive, with the forward car of which the offending axle was a part, rolled off to the repair shop. Then a voice was raised. "Father Abraham! Father Abraham! Come forth! Your children want to see you." The crowd gave way, and the minister of the village Lutheran church, one Rev. Alleman, continuing his appeal, stepped close to the coach. A moment later Lincoln's tall figure appeared in the doorway. Stooping so that the crown of his head would clear the lintel, he strode out on the platform, smiled sadly, and slowly descended the lower step.

I was close by. In order that I might touch the skirts of Lincoln's coat, I squirmed beneath the coach and wriggled between its wheels, and as I emerged my shoulder brushed the President's knee. The great, kindly face looked down at me and again smiled wistfully, and the great, friendly hand patted my proud, happy head. Thrilled and strangely moved, I forthwith made up my mind to go to Gettysburg the next day, even though I should have to walk. With his eyes still fixed on me Lincoln began to speak; and while he spoke his thoughts seemed to be far away and unrelated to the words he uttered, for that day his mountainous troubles were peaked by a distressing anxiety due to the critical condition of his little son Tad.

After thanking the townspeople for being good enough to greet him, he referred to the fight which had taken place at Hanover on the day before the opening of the Battle of Gettysburg as the "prelude to one of the world's most momentous battles." He said it was his opinion that had not General Jeb Stuart been engaged by general Kilpatrick at Hanover and as a result been turned east, General Lee would have had the support, from the very beginning of the conflict at Gettysburg, of his best-trained and most effective cavalry forces under the command of his ablest general.

Scarcely had the train departed when two of my brothers and I sought out our father and succeeded in arranging for the use of our old family mare next day. Early the following morning we were on our way. When we reached Gettysburg there was a parade in progress. Astride a large sorrel horse, Lincoln rode well forward in the procession,

preceded by Colonel Graham and his Fifth New York Regiment of Artillery, and followed by an escort made up of
Chief Marshal Ward H. Lamon, General Wright, General
Doubleday, General Mason, and their staffs. In the van of
the parade was a brass band; scattered through its length
of less than a quarter mile were lodge delegations, regiments of cavalry and artillery, and other brass bands,
while a host of folk from the surrounding countryside
brought up the rear.

Becoming separated from my brothers, I hastened to
the spot about to be dedicated as a national cemetery.
There I hid under the speaker's stand. Finally, when the
parade had reached the cemetery and had disbanded and
the platform was heavy with personages, official and un-
official, and Christ Church choir, which was ranged along
the one side, began to chant, I discovered the whereabouts
of Lincoln and stationed myself at the feet of my hero.
Through a crack between the planks I could look directly
into Lincoln's face. Its deep lines, the wrinkled brow, the
deep-set brooding eyes burned indelible images into my
memory. Now, although a man of eighty-five, I still feel
keenly those tuggings at the heartstrings which seized me
that autumn day when I gazed into the face of the President who knew more trials and tribulations than any
other of our Chief Executives.

The pause that had followed the prayer by Dr. Stock-
ton, chaplain of the House of Representatives, now gave
way to stirrings-about above. I shifted my position to another crack close to the front of the platform. Edward
Everett was unfolding the manuscript of his oration; but I
was not interested. I returned to my former position. Until
Edward Everett began to speak the President gazed into
space; and then, as the first period of that ornate oration,

which was to consume an hour and twenty minutes, was uttered, he leaned from one side to the other and crossed his legs, turning his eyes full upon the speaker. Somewhat later he again shifted his position and rested his chin in the palm of his right hand. His eyes now wandered over the audience. Frequently he swallowed hard and tears welled as he spied the black weeds of some bereft mother or widow.

When Edward Everett finished speaking, Lincoln slowly took his hand from his chin, bent slightly forward, and very deliberately drew from an inner pocket of his coat a few flimsy pieces of paper. These he shuffled from hand to hand until the particular sheet he was seeking appeared. Leaning back in the chair again, but without recrossing his legs, he intently studied what he had written on that sheet. The posture was characteristic, and some sculptor has long since given it permanency in bronze. Tucking away the papers, he arose, and very slowly stepped to the front of the platform. The flutter and motion of the crowd ceased the moment the President was on his feet. Such was the quiet that his footfalls, I remember very distinctly, woke echoes, and with the creaking of the boards, it was as if someone were walking through the hallways of an empty house.

The crack through which for a moment or two I had glanced at Edward Everett I now found to be of no use, for Lincoln had stationed himself just a little in front of it, and only his coat tails were visible. An instant later, to my great relief, he stepped back a pace or two and again I could look up into that sad face with its furrowed brow. The brooding eyes now glowed with a strange light such as is sometimes provoked by a fever. Then Lincoln began to speak. Word followed word so slowly that the value of each syllable was unduly magnified. "Fourscore and seven years ago our forefathers brought forth upon this continent a new nation"—here there was a decided pause; this pause I well remember because I held my breath, wondering what had happened to cause it—"conceived in liberty"—another pause and more high emphasis, this time on the word "liberty"—"and dedicated to the proposition that all men are created equal."

Beginning with the next sentence he spoke more rapidly, but somewhere near the middle of the address he slowed again to the tempo of the opening words.

Now the group of Negroes off to one side, that had been wailing "Amens" in an undertone, lifted their voices higher and higher as the simple eloquence of Lincoln moved them. A number of them were weeping; others with closed eyes repeated phrases of the address. The deep resonant voice continued: ". . . whether that nation, or any nation, so conceived and so dedicated, can long endure." These words were spoken very slowly indeed. With the next sentence he quickened his delivery, and when he came to "gave the last full measure of devotion," tears trickled down his cheeks, and I could not help some welling up in my own eyes.

Then he cleared his throat. With a large white handkerchief, which he drew from the inner pocket of his coat and allowed to dangle for a moment from his right hand, he brushed away the tears and mopped his brow, and for the first time, as I remember, shifted his feet. During the final phrases of the address I was thrilled as I had not been by all the previous sentences. It was certainly not what he said that made me feel so, but the way and manner of his saying it.

With the address finished, the assemblage stood motionless and silent. The heads of many were bowed as were those of the Negroes, who now, with a long and solemn "Amen," were the only ones to disturb the stillness. The extreme brevity of the address together with its abrupt close had so astonished the hearers that they stood transfixed. Had not Lincoln turned and moved toward his chair, the audience would very likely have remained voiceless for several moments more. Finally there came applause and a calling, "Yes! Yes! Government for the people!" It was as if the Blue Ridge Mountains to the west were echoing Lincoln's concluding and keynote thought.

Edward Everett was the first to approach the President and shake hands with him. He said with feeling that Lincoln's few eloquent words had been written upon the memory of man and would endure, while his own were only for the moment. The others of importance who had been seated well forward on the platform, now surrounded the President. Noticing that some of the Christ Church choir members were trying to approach him, he waved aside the notables and began to shake hands with the singers.

Among them was a girl of fifteen, several years younger than any of the others, Louisa Vandersloot. He had heard her high, clear soprano voice; he motioned her toward him. Leaning over two of the older choristers, he extended his long arm and, as she puts it, "his great, warm, all-enveloping hand took hold of my little one and almost crushed it." That evening, during a reception, the President again singled out this girl and once more crushed her tender fingers with his great hand. She is now a woman of almost my age—Mrs. M. O. Smith; and frequently we exchange reminiscences of the Day of the Dedication. She, just as I, fairly felt his kindliness and greatness of soul and "tingled all over" when he held her close to him.

Meanwhile I and my brothers, whom I found at the back of the platform, made our way to the edge of the crowd, and among the huge rocks with which that part of the battlefield was still covered in spots we scrambled until we reached the highway leading to town. Over its dusty course we hurried to the home of Judge Wills, which stood on a corner of the village green. It was there that Lincoln was being entertained; and I felt sure that the judge, a friend of my father, would see to it that we got to shake hands with Lincoln.

We entered the Wills home by way of the kitchen. The judge and the President had just driven up to the front door and were having trouble to explain to a crowd that there would be no reception before evening. When we ventured into the front hall, the judge had closed the door and was asking Lincoln whether he cared to lunch then or an hour later. The President said he was not hungry and wanted to rest. Just as he was about to go upstairs we boys stepped out of a dusky corner. The judge immediately recognized us and smiled.

"Well, how did you fellows get in here?" he inquired. "I think I know what you want. I'm sure the President will shake hands with you. Here, Mr. President, are the sons of an old friend of mine. They have come over from Hanover to see you."

Without hesitation the President turned and shook hands with each of us, remarking that he was greatly pleased that we had thought it worthwhile to journey to Gettysburg and help with our presence in the dedication of the battlefield. Then, putting an arm around me and a hand on my younger brother's shoulder, he added: "The fight in your town must have furnished you fellows considerable excitement. Maybe more than you cared for." These words I remember as vividly as if they had been spoken only yesterday.

He then said something about hoping the war would soon end so that no more young men would have to be called to the front. With great emotion and with tears in his eyes he spoke of all the heartaches and the pangs that all the horror of the war caused him. "May the whole terrible thing soon end," he murmured as he turned away from us. As he started to ascend the stairs he sighed deeply and cleared his throat. A moment later he disappeared into the shadows that enveloped the upper reaches of the stairway.

"Tears rolled down on Lincoln's coat-sleeve"

Lincoln's sympathy for his soldiers is shown in this account written by Dr. Francis Dubin Blakeslee.

LINCOLN used to visit the hospitals. His great, sympathizing heart impelled him to seek to comfort the sick, the wounded and often dying boys of the army. He had been at one hospital nearly all day with a company of friends. Just as they were entering their carriages to leave, an attendant rushed out and said to one of the party: "There is a Confederate prisoner in one of the wards that the president did not visit, and he wants to see the President." When Lincoln was told, he said, "I'll go back." As he approached the cot and extended his hand, the young fellow exclaimed: "I knew they were mistaken!" He had heard all that talk about the ape, the baboon, the gorilla; but one glance at the kindly face dispelled it all and he said: "I knew they were mistaken!"

"What can I do for you, young man?" inquired Lincoln. "Oh, I don't know anybody up here, and the surgeon tells me I can't live, and I wanted to see you before I die." The President asked him about his father, mother, his brothers and his sisters. The young fellow's confidence was won, and he told about his family and his home; about his keep-

[From Rufus R. Wilson, *Intimate Memories of Lincoln*, Elmira, N.Y., 1945]

sakes and what he wanted done with them. Lincoln listened sympathetically and promised to see that a letter
was written. He still tarried, trying to prepare the young
man for "the great adventure." Presently he said: "Now,
my boy, I have been here nearly all day. I am a very busy
man and I ought to be going; but is there anything more
that I can do for you?" "I was hoping you would stay and
see me through." And the great tears rolled down on Lincoln's coat-sleeve as he continued to minister to the dying
boy.

"Would you . . . shake hands with me if I were to tell you who I am?"

In 1862 Lincoln went to Maryland to visit the Army of the Potomac. He appeared at a rebel hospital in Sharpsburg. The following piece was written by a Baltimore newspaperman who observed Lincoln there.

PASSING through one of the hospitals devoted exclusively to Confederate sick and wounded, President Lincoln's attention was drawn to a young Georgian—a fine noble-looking youth—stretched upon a humble cot. He was pale, emaciated and anxious, far from kindred and home, vibrating, as it were, between life and death. Every stranger that entered [was] caught in his restless eyes, in hope of their being some relative or friend. President Lincoln observed this youthful soldier, approached and spoke, asking him if he suffered much pain. "I do," was the reply. "I have lost a leg, and feel I am sinking from exhaustion." "Would you," said Mr. Lincoln, "shake hands with me if I were to tell you who I am?" The response was affirmative. "There should," remarked the young Georgian, "be no enemies in this place." Then said the distinguished visitor, "I am Abraham Lincoln, President of the United States." The young sufferer raised his head, looking amazed, and

[From the *New York Herald*, October 3, 1862]

freely extended his hand, which Mr. Lincoln took and pressed tenderly for some time. There followed an instinctive pause. The wounded Confederate's eyes melted into tears, his lips quivered, and his heart beat full. President Lincoln bent over him motionless and dumb. His eyes, too, were overflowing, thus giving utterance to emotions far beyond the power of any language to describe. It was a most touching scene. Not a dry eye was present. Silence was subsequently broken by a kind conciliatory conversation between the President and this young Confederate, when they parted there being but slim hope of the latter's recovery.

"You are justly entitled to one of your boys"

This account of a mother's plea for her son and Lincoln's re-sponse was told by a reporter for the Washington Republican *named Murtaugh and published in* Six Months at the White House.

I WAS waiting my turn to speak to the President one day ... when my attention was attracted by the sad patient face of a woman advanced in life, who in a faded hood and shawl was among the applicants for an interview.

Presently Mr. Lincoln turned to her, saying in his accustomed manner, "Well, my good woman, what can I do for you this morning?" "Mr. President," said she, "my husband and three sons all went into the army. My husband was killed in the fight at——. I get along very badly since then, living all alone, and I thought I would come and ask you to release my oldest son." Mr. Lincoln looked into her face a moment, and in his kindest accents responded, "Certainly! Certainly! If you have given us *all*, and your prop has been taken away, you are justly entitled to one of your boys!" He immediately made out an order discharging the young man, which the woman took, and thanking him gratefully, went away.

[From Francis B. Carpenter, *Six Months at the White House with Abraham Lincoln*, New York, 1866]

I had forgotten the circumstance . . . till last week, when happening to be here again, who should come in but the same woman. It appeared that she had gone herself to the front, with the President's order, and found the son she was in search of had been mortally wounded in a recent engagement, and taken to a hospital. She found the hospital, but the boy was dead, or died while she was there. The surgeon in charge made a memorandum of the facts upon the back of the President's order, and almost broken-hearted, the poor woman had found her way again into Mr. Lincoln's presence. He was much affected by her appearance and story, and said: "I know what you wish me to do now, and I shall do it without your asking; I shall release to you your second son." Upon this, he took up his pen and commenced writing the order. While he was writing the poor woman stood by his side, the tears running down her face, and passed her hand softly over his head, stroking his rough hair, as I have seen a fond mother caress a son. By the time he had finished writing, his own heart and eyes were full. He handed her the paper: "Now," said he, "*you* have one and *I* have one of the other two left: that is no more than right." She took the paper, and reverently placing her hand again upon his head, the tears still upon her cheeks, said: "The Lord bless you, Mr. Lincoln. May you live a thousand years, and may you always be the head of this great nation!"

"Without 'oath,' condition, or reserve"

Lincoln was particularly sympathetic to those who had been injured during the war.

THE Hon. Orlando Kellogg, of New York, was sitting in his room at his boarding-house one evening, when one of his constituents appeared,—a white-headed old man,—who had come to Washington in great trouble, to seek the aid of his representative in behalf of his son. His story was this: during an absence from home a year or two previous to the war, he enlisted in the regular army, and, after serving six months, deserted. Returning to his father, who knew nothing of this, he reformed his habits, and when the war broke out, entered heart and soul into the object of raising a regiment in his native country, and was subsequently elected one of its officers. He had proved an efficient officer, distinguishing himself particularly on one occasion in a charge across a bridge, when he was severely wounded,—his colonel being killed by his side. Shortly after this, he came in contact with one of his old companions in the "regular" service, who recognized him, and declared his purpose of informing against him. Overwhelmed with mortification, the young man procured a furlough

[From Francis B. Carpenter, *Six Months at the White House with Abraham Lincoln*, New York, 1866]

and returned home, revealing the matter to his father, and declaring his purpose never to submit to an arrest,—"he would die first." In broken tones the old man finished his statement, saying: "Can you do anything for us, Judge?— it is a hard, hard, case!" "I will see about that," replied the representative, putting on his hat; "wait here until I return." He went immediately to the White House, and fortunately finding Mr. Lincoln alone, they sat down together, and he repeated the old man's story. The President made no demonstration of particular interest until the Judge reached the description of the charge across the bridge, and the wound received. "Do you say," he interrupted, "that the young man was wounded?" "Yes," replied the congressman, "badly." "Then he has shed his blood for his country," responded Mr. Lincoln, musingly. "Kellogg," he continued, brightening up, "isn't there something in Scripture about the 'shedding of blood' being 'the remission of sins?'" "Guess you are about right there," replied the Judge. "It is a good 'point,' and there is no going behind it," rejoined the President; and taking up his pen, another "pardon"—this time without "oath," condition, or reserve—was added to the records of the War Office.

"Leg cases"

Schuyler Colfax, a congressman from Indiana and later Speaker of the House, wrote this account of Lincoln's mercy.

FINALLY, there was a very flagrant case of a soldier who, in the crisis of a battle, demoralized his regiment by his cowardice, throwing down his gun and hiding behind the friendly stump. When tried for his cowardice there was no defense. The court-martial, in examining his antecedents, found that he had neither father nor mother living, nor wife nor child; that he was unfit to wear the loyal uniform, and that he was a thief who stole continually from his comrades. "Here," said Judge Holt, "is a case which comes exactly within your requirements. He does not deny his guilt; he will better serve the country dead than living, as he has no relations to mourn for him, and he is not fit to be in the ranks of patriots, at any rate." Mr. Lincoln's refuge of excuse was all swept away. Judge Holt expected, of course, that he would write "approved" on the paper; but the President, running his long fingers through his hair, as he so often used to do when in anxious thought, replied, "Well, after all, Judge, I think I must put him with my leg cases."

[From Allen Thorndike Rice, ed., *Reminiscences of Abraham Lincoln by Distinguished Men of His Time*, New York, 1886]

"*Leg cases*," said Judge Holt, with a frown at this supposed levity of the President, in a case of life and death. "What do you mean by *leg cases*, sir?"

"Why, why," replied Mr. Lincoln, "do you see those papers crowded into those pigeon-holes? They are the cases that you call by that long title, 'cowardice in the face of the enemy,' but I call them, for short, my 'leg cases.' But I put it to you, and I leave it for you to decide for yourself: if Almighty God gives a man a cowardly pair of legs, how can he help their running away with him?"

Let me give another anecdote bearing on the same subject. A Congressman went up to the White House one morning on business, and saw in the anteroom, always crowded with people in those days, an old man, crouched all alone in a corner, crying as if his heart would break. As such a sight was by no means uncommon, the Congressman passed into the President's room, transacted his business, and went away. The next morning he was obliged again to go to the White House, and he saw the same old man crying, as before, in the corner. He stopped, and said to him, "What's the matter with you, old man?" The old man told him the story of his son; that he was a soldier in the Army of the James—General Butler's army—that he had been convicted by a court-martial of an outrageous crime and sentenced to be shot next week; and that his Congressman was so convinced of the convicted man's guilt that he would not intervene. "Well," said Mr. Alley, "I will take you into the Executive Chamber after I have finished my business, and you can tell Mr. Lincoln all about it. On being introduced into Mr. Lincoln's presence, he was accosted with, "Well, my old friend, what can I do for you to-day?" The old man then repeated to Mr. Lincoln what he had already told the Congressman in the anteroom. A cloud of sorrow came over the President's face as he replied, "I am sorry to say I can do nothing for you. Listen to this telegram received from General Butler yesterday: 'President Lincoln, I pray you not to interfere with the courts-martial of the army. You will destroy all discipline among our soldiers.'—B. F. Butler."

Every word of this dispatch seemed like the death-knell of despair to the old man's newly awakened hopes. Mr. Lincoln watched his grief for a minute, and then exclaimed, "By jingo, Butler or no Butler, here goes!"— writing a few words and handing them to the old man. The confidence created by Mr. Lincoln's words broke down when he read—"Job Smith is not to be shot until further orders from me.—ABRAHAM LINCOLN."

"Why," said the old man, "I thought it was to be a pardon; but you say, 'not to be shot till further orders,' and you may order him to be shot next week." Mr. Lincoln smiled at the old man's fears, and replied, "Well, my old friend, I see you are not very well acquainted with me. If your son never looks on death till further orders come from me to shoot him, he will live to be a great deal older than Methuselah."

"Inexpressible sympathy and goodness"

In this account, Mrs. Anna Byers-Jennings not only receives a pardon for a friend, she receives an invitation to supper.

IN OCTOBER, 1864, I went from Fairmont, Missouri, to Washington City, in behalf of Daniel Hayden of Scotland County, who had been captured at Helena, Arkansas, fifteen months before, and who was now confined in the old Alton, Illinois, penitentiary, which had been turned into a military prison.

On the train I met Colonel Thomas Turner of Freeport, Illinois, and Colonel Hancock of Chicago, president of the board of trade. Colonel Turner, who was a longtime friend, informed me that they were going to Washington on a most delightful mission. The Union League of Chicago had passed very complimentary resolutions in favor of Mr. Lincoln upon his renomination, and these two gentlemen had been chosen by the league to present them in person to the President. . . .

At the entrance (to the White House) I met an old man, a clerk in the department of the commissary-general of prisoners—Colonel William Hoffman's department. I had accidentally met and conversed with the plain old fellow, who proved my salvation at this time.

[From Rufus R. Wilson, *Lincoln Among His Friends*, Caldwell, Idaho, 1942]

The moment he met me he said: "Have you seen the President yet?"

I replied in the negative. He then advised me to go right up. He said: "It is now past office hours. I have just left the President; went in to get these papers signed. To-morrow the cabinet meets; the next day is Sunday, Monday is always a busy day, so you cannot hope to see him before Tuesday evening, even though you were first on the list, and there are hundreds ahead of you."

I certainly felt that the old man's advice was good, but it also occurred to me that I would be running a great risk to walk into the private office of President Lincoln, unannounced and uncalled for. I was only a green young woman from the backwoods of Missouri. What would I do if he should order me out, or something of that kind? My case would surely be hopeless and I undone. But the thought of the poor old father who was paying my expenses, and the advice of the clerk whom I met made me somewhat desperate, and after getting up all the courage possible I made my way upstairs and to the door of the office. I could feel my heart beating in an unusual manner, and I was actually trembling from head to foot. At last I took hold of the door knob, hesitated a moment, then turned it and walked in.

Mr. Lincoln was all alone, sitting beside a very plain table, resting his elbow on the table, and his head upon his hand. . . .

When I entered he raised his tired eyes, oh so tired, and with a worn look I can never, never forget. As I advanced, and before he spoke, I said: "Mr. Lincoln, you must pardon this intrusion, but I just could not wait any longer to see you." The saintly man then reached out his friendly hand and said: "No intrusion at all, not the least. Sit down, my child, sit down, and let me know what I can do for you." I suggested that probably he was too tired. He replied: "I am tired, but I am waiting to say good-bye to two friends from Chicago who are going on the train at seven."

I briefly explained to him the case before me, saying that Hayden had been in prison fifteen months; that he was a Union man, forced from his home by the rebels; that his wife had died since he had been in prison, leaving five little children with his very aged mother, who had lately lost her eyesight. I had, besides, a large envelope filled with letters of recommendation from different officers of the Department of Missouri; also a petition drawn up by myself, signed by the Union neighbors of Mr. Hayden; appended to it a certificate of their loyalty, signed by the county clerk, Wallace Permott, who had affixed the seal of the county court. To all of the above Senator John B. Henderson had been kind enough to add an indorsement for myself, in strong, impressive language.

When I offered my papers to the President he didn't touch them, but said, without raising a hand: "Now, suppose you read them over for me. Your eyes are younger than mine. Besides, as I told you, I am very, very tired." By accident, the petition was the first thing I took up. When I came to John B. Henderson's name he reached out and said quickly: "Let me see that." As he glanced over it to the bottom, he laid the paper down, slapped his hand upon the table and exclaimed: "Plague on me, if that ain't John Henderson's signature. Well, I'll release this man just because John Henderson asks me to do it. I know he wouldn't ask me if it wasn't right, nor send any one here that would do anything detrimental to our government. Come in tomorrow at 8 o'clock—mind, at 8 precisely. Bring that petition with John Henderson's name on it and I'll fix it so you can get this man out of prison." He then seemed interested and asked me several questions about men and matters in Northeast Missouri.

At this moment the door opened and Colonels Turner and Hancock entered. He greeted them in a very off-hand manner, motioned them to seats, then turning to Colonel Turner, he said: "Why, this must be the young woman you told me about." At this the very gallant, elegant looking man immediately stood up and in a most gracious manner said: "Yes, Mr. Lincoln, this is the daughter of an old friend of mine, and I beg you may hear what she has to say, and grant her request for my sake."

"All right, Colonel, all right. Sit down."

Our mingled conversation lasted about half an hour. As we were rising to leave Mr. Lincoln, addressing all three, said: "Now you folks have come with your favors to bestow and petitions to be granted. I have promised to do all that has been asked of me, and said the finest things I could to what has been bestowed. So I think I ought to have my way next, and what I have to ask is that you all three come and eat dinner with me to-morrow. Will you do it?" Of course, we accepted with profuse thanks, and as we said good-bye he reminded us: "No formality at dinner tomorrow. Not a bit." At this moment I remembered and said: "Now, Mr. Lincoln, you have requested me to be here at 8 o'clock in the morning. Pray tell me how I am to get in?" "Oh, the usher is only a slender little Irishman. If he refuses to let you pass, slap him down the steps, and walk in as you did just now." At this the gentlemen all laughed heartily and, as the President turned to me, he held out his hand, and smiling like summer, said: "You come when

I tell you, my child, and you'll get in as sure as you're alive."

I walked briskly to the White House the next morning and stood at the head of the stairs, waiting for my watch to say the moment, not in the least guessing how I was to get permission to enter. Standing at the end of the corridor nearest to the door I had passed through the day before, I heard some one say: "This way, Mrs. Byers." Looking up I saw, to my great astonishment, at the farther end of the corridor, the President motioning for me to come. I walked up to where he stood as quickly as possible. He grasped my hand warmly, led me in and introduced me to William H. Seward and Mr. Nicolay. He sat down by his desk, reached out for the petition, wrote across the back, "Release this man on order No. —. A. Lincoln." As he handed it straight back to me he remarked with looks full of inexpressible sympathy and goodness: "Mrs. Byers, that will get your man out. And tell his poor old mother I wish to heaven it was in my power to give her back her eyesight so she might see her son when he gets home to her."

That afternoon we went together from Willard's Hotel to dine with President Lincoln, and of all informal affairs I have ever attended, it certainly took the lead. I was seated at the right of the President, Colonel Turner on his left. Mrs. Lincoln, the two boys and Colonel Hancock occupied the rest of the table. When a dish of anything was brought, he reached out for it, handled the spoon like an ordinary farmer, saying to all in his reach: "Will you have some of this?" dishing it into our plates liberally. And so it was throughout the whole dinner, as he said, truly informal. Mrs. Lincoln was very sweet and gracious. The contrast between them was so striking that I have them plainly before me this moment as they appeared then.

I have always considered the President's action through this whole affair of my own very extraordinary in more ways than one. Mr. Lincoln was at this time President of the United States and commander-in-chief of her armies—no foreign nations to contend with, but his own beloved land and country. So many, many wonderfully weighty matters upon his heart, mind and hands, and yet to remember that I, an ordinary woman on an ordinary mission, had been promised admission at 8 o'clock on the morning of the 8th of October, and that this small matter had not been forgotten. Stranger than all, that he had not forgotten the poor, blind mother.

The more I contemplate the character of Abraham Lincoln, the more I find to admire, and the more I am convinced that it is beyond the power of mortals to portray the many God-like characteristics of this, the chief of all created men.

"You don't wear hoops"

Lincoln's desire to help the young girl in this account may have been influenced by his seeing in her a kindred soul.

LIEUTENANT-GOVERNOR Ford, of Ohio, had an appointment with [Lincoln] one evening at six o'clock. As he entered the vestibule of the White House his attention was attracted by a poorly clad young woman who was violently sobbing. He asked her the cause of her distress. She said that she had been ordered away by the servants, after vainly waiting many hours to see the President about her only brother, who had been condemned to death. Her story was this: she and her brother were foreigners, and orphans. They had been in this country several years. Her brother enlisted in the army, but, through bad influences, was induced to desert. He was captured, tried, and sentenced to be shot—the old story. The poor girl had obtained the signatures of some persons who had formerly known him to petition for a pardon, and, alone, had come to Washington to lay the case before the President. Thronged as the waiting-rooms always were, she had passed the long hours of two days trying in vain to get an audience, and had at length been ordered away.

[From Francis B. Carpenter, *Six Months at the White House with Abraham Lincoln*, New York, 1866]

Mr. Ford's sympathies were at once enlisted. He said that he had come to see the President, but did not know as *he* should succeed. He told her, however, to follow him upstairs, and he would see what could be done. Just before reaching the door, Mr. Lincoln came out, and meeting his friend, said good-humoredly, "are you not ahead of time?" Mr. Ford showed his watch, with the pointers upon the hour of six. "Well," replied Mr. Lincoln, "I have not had time to get a lunch. Go in and sit down; I will be back directly."

Mr. Ford made the young woman accompany him into the office, and when they were seated, said to her: "Now, my good girl, I want you to muster all the courage you have in the world. When the President comes back he will sit down in that arm-chair. I shall get up to speak to him, and as I do so you must force yourself between us, and insist upon his examination of your papers, telling him it is a case of life and death, and admits of no delay." These instructions were carried out to the letter. Mr. Lincoln was at first somewhat surprised at the apparent forwardness of the young woman, but observing her distressed appearance, he ceased conversation with his friend, and commenced an examination of the document she had placed in his hands. Glancing from it to the face of the petitioner, whose tears had broken forth afresh, he studied its expression for a moment, and then his eye fell upon her scanty but neat dress. Instantly his face lighted up. "My poor girl," said he, "you have come here with no governor, or senator, or member of congress, to plead your cause. You seem honest and truthful; and"—with much emphasis—"you don't wear '*hoops*'; and I will be whipped but I will pardon your brother!"

"So much worse than the most depraved murderer"

Written by Lincoln's friend and bodyguard Ward Hill Lamon, this account shows that not everyone who came to ask for mercy received it.

THE following incident will illustrate another phase of Mr. Lincoln's character. A man who was then in jail at Newburyport, Massachusetts, as a convicted slave-trader, and who had been fined one thousand dollars and sentenced to imprisonment for five years, petitioned for a pardon. The petition was accompanied by a letter to the Hon. John B. Alley, a member of Congress from Lynn, Massachusetts. Mr. Alley presented the papers to the President, with a letter from the prisoner acknowledging his guilt and the justice of his sentence. He had served out the term of sentence of imprisonment, but was still held on account of the fine not being paid. Mr. Lincoln was much moved by the pathetic appeal. He then, after pausing some time, said to Mr. Alley: "My friend, this appeal is very touching to my feelings, and no one knows my weakness better than you. It is, if possible, to be too easily moved by appeals for mercy; and I must say that if this

[From Ward Hill Lamon, _Recollections of Abraham Lincoln, 1847–1865_, Chicago, 1895]

man had been guilty of the foulest murder that the arm of man could perpetrate, I might forgive him on such an appeal. But the man who could go to Africa and rob her of her children, and then sell them into interminable bondage, with no other motive than that which is furnished by dollars and cents, is so much worse than the most depraved murderer that he can never receive pardon at my hand. No, sir; he may stay in jail forever before he shall have liberty by any act of mine."

Part Four

LINCOLN'S KINDNESS

YOU prepare to take your leave of the president, your heart aching with gratitude as you realize the immense debt you owe him. You try to convey to him your gratefulness, but words fall short. You thank him for his time. You wonder why this man, with the weight of the nation's agony on his shoulders, has taken the time to see you and the others who today had lined up to see him. With a warm handshake you leave Lincoln's office, convinced that this one man is indeed the true embodiment of the best of America.

"The story of a little girl"

This account was written by Hannah Slater Jacobs, who, when she met President Lincoln, was a young girl. After learning that her father's job with the government was being unfairly threatened, she told her father to go see President Lincoln. When her father refused, she decided, with "courage born of despair," to go see him herself.

. . . BRIGHT and early . . . I was up and dressed in my best Sunday frock, my hair carefully braided, with my prettiest hair-ribbons and hat; and leaving word that I had gone out to do an errand, I started for the White House.

The streets seemed quiet and I wondered why. It was late in May, and the sun was high so it did not occur to me that it was still early. I had quite a walk to the White House and when I reached there, no one seemed to be around. I went up through the great portico to the front door and rang the bell. After what seemed to me a long wait, a tall doorkeeper opened the door, and, looking much surprised to see me standing there, said bruskly, "What do you want?"

"If you please, sir, I should like to see the President."

[From Hannah Slater Jacobs, "Mr. Lincoln Gives Heed to a Young Girl's Story," *Good Housekeeping*, February 1932]

He looked at me in amazement. "Well," he said, "you certainly are making an early call. Don't you know the doors aren't open until nine o'clock?"

"No, sir," I replied, "I am a stranger here, and I don't know anything about your rules and regulations, and I haven't any idea what time it is."

"Well," he answered, "the President isn't even up yet, and anyway he's not receiving visitors these days. For two or three weeks he has not seen any one except on urgent business."

"Oh!" I exclaimed, "my business is important! I *must* see him. My father is an Army officer and in trouble, and I must tell the President about it."

"Well," he replied, "if the President could see you, it would not be before eleven o'clock, and it's not seven yet. You would have a long wait, should he see you at all, which I think is doubtful. Do you live far from here?"

"Yes sir, I do."

"Well, which would you rather do, go home and come back, wait outdoors, or—would you like to come in?"

"If you please," I said, "I would like to come in."

"Very well," he decided, "you may go up to the second floor into the reception room; but remember, I don't believe you can see the President."

I went up as he directed and looked about the room, and out of the windows, enjoying especially the views out over the lovely grounds. By and by I began to hear stirrings above me and I decided the President must be getting up. After a long time I went across the hall and looked out of the front windows and saw crowds of people coming from every direction. At last the doors were opened, and by ten o'clock the rooms upstairs and down were packed. It was a distinguished-looking company; all the Army and

Navy officers with gilt braid and buttons, and foreign diplomats in full regalia, and fashionably-dressed women. And how anxious they all were to see the President! I heard one lady say:

"I have been coming here every day for three weeks hoping to see Mr. Lincoln, and have not succeeded in having an interview with him yet."

Another replied: "I have been coming every day for weeks without being able to see him. I want my son transferred from one hospital to another, and the authorities won't do it. I know if I could see President Lincoln for five minutes he would grant my request."

So one after another I heard these people telling of their daily disappointment, and I began to feel pretty hopeless. I was only a little girl; this was my first visit, and I knew I could never get up sufficient courage to come again if I failed this time. I had just about decided I had better go, when I saw the tall doorkeeper come in, looking all about for some one. There were Generals and Admirals, and all sorts of important-looking personages, and I supposed he was trying to find one of them. But suddenly I saw him beckoning to me. I looked at him questioningly, and he nodded. I went to him and he whispered, "You may see the President now."

How can I describe my feelings? It seemed too good to be true, and yet, in spite of my happiness, I was so frightened I could scarcely move. I mustered up courage, however, to follow him. He opened a door and pushed me in: and there I was—all alone with the President.

Mr. Lincoln was sitting in an armchair in the farthest corner of the room. Seeing my timidity, he rose, and beckoning in a friendly way said: "Come this way, Sis; come this way."

His voice was so kind and gentle that all my fright left me immediately. He came in great strides to meet me, and taking me by the hand, welcomed me most cordially. "And did you wish to see me?" he inquired.

"Yes, Mr. President," I replied, "My father is in trouble and I have come to tell you about it."

"Does your father know you have come?"

"Oh, no, Mr. President. He would not have allowed me to come if he had known anything about it. I wanted him to come, himself, to see you, but he said you were too burdened for him to trouble you, and he would not come. I stayed awake all last night thinking about his trouble and decided I would come myself. So before he was up, I slipped out of the house without his knowledge."

A kindly smile lighted President Lincoln's face and he said: "Come sit down and tell me all about it."

His sympathy made me feel at ease, and I told him all the story in detail. When I was telling him of Father's being wounded at the Battle of Fredericksburg and of the necessity of the amputation of his leg, and of his and Mother's sufferings, he interrupted me. "So your father was wounded at Fredericksburg?" he said.

"Yes, Mr. President," I answered.

He threw his head back on the chair, and as he clasped his hands before him and closed his eyes, a look of agony passed over his face. With a groan, he said: "Oh, what a terrible slaughter that was! Those dreadful days! Shall I ever forget them? No, never, never." Then recovering himself, he said: "Go on, my child, go on."

So I went on and told him all about our leaving our old home; of Father's appointment to Chain Bridge and of the indignity he had suffered; of his anxiety concerning the welfare of his big family; and how, only the day before, the Division Commander had seemed to threaten his removal.

When I was all through, the President said: "My child, every day I am obliged to listen to many stories such as yours. How am I to know what you have told me is true?"

"I'm sure I don't know, Mr. President," I replied, "unless you are willing to take my word for it."

"That's just what I'm going to do," he said as he patted me on the shoulder. "I will thoroughly investigate this affair," and taking a notebook from his pocket, he made a memorandum of what I had told him. Then closing the book, he said: "Now, my child, you go home and tell your father not to worry any more about this. I will look into the matter myself, and I will see to it personally that no further injustice is done him. He can rest assured that he will either be retained in his present position or have a better one. It will come out all right, I can promise you."

Grasping his hand in both of mine, all I could say was: "Thank you so much, Mr. President."

"That's all right, my child, all right." And then rising he bade me good-bye with all the graciousness he would have shown some notable woman, and bowed me out.

I stood for a moment fairly dazed. How unbelievably marvelous it all seemed, and what a wonderful man our President was!

I fairly walked on air all the way home, and I could hardly wait for Father's return that evening. At last I saw him coming on his crutches, care-worn and worried. Mother met him at the door with the usual question, "Well, Father, how have things gone today?"

"No better, Mother," he answered sadly.

Then I could restrain myself no longer and cried out, "It's all right, Father! Everything is going to be all right!"

"What's all right, child? What do you mean?"

"Well," I said, so happy that I could scarcely talk coherently, "I went to the White House today and saw the President and told him all about your trouble—"

"You went to see the President!" he interrupted, "What on earth did you do that for? I never dreamed of your doing such a thing! The President never heard of me. He doesn't know a thing about me. Why should he be troubled with my affairs?"

"Well," I replied, "you refused to go to him because you said you would not bother him with your troubles; so I went to him, myself. I told him all about it, and I have a message for you from Mr. Lincoln. He told me to tell you not to worry one bit more, that he would investigate the matter personally and you should either keep your present position or have a better one."

The expression on my father's face was a study. Bewilderment, amazement, incredulity, and joy were all mingled.

"Did I ever!" he cried. "Bless your heart!"

Gathering me in his arms he held me close, struggling to keep back the tears that were threatening.

The President kept his word. He did just what he said he would. In a few days, when the General made his next visit to the station, he was as courteous as he could be to Father.

"Good morning, Captain," he said, and came to Father's desk to transact business with him for the first time.

And after that, in all their relations, there was never the slightest shadow of unpleasantness.

I never saw the President to speak to him again. Within two years he was dead, and our hearts grieved as if he had been one of our own. But down through the years I have had this memory of the big-hearted, sympathetic man, burdened by affairs of state, beset by hundreds of people, as he sat patiently, unhurriedly, listening to the story of a little girl.

"I felt that I was in the presence of a friend"

Well over eighty, Sojourner Truth, the courageous and revered abolitionist leader, decided she must see the President before she died. She dictated to a friend this account of her visit.

IT WAS about eight o'clock, A.M., when I called on the President. Upon entering his reception-room we found about a dozen persons in waiting, among them two colored women. I had quite a pleasant time waiting until he was disengaged, and enjoyed his conversation with others; he showed as much kindness and consideration to the colored persons as to the whites,—if there was any difference, more. One case was that of a colored woman, who was sick and likely to be turned out of her house on account of her inability to pay her rent. The President listened to her with much attention, and spoke to her with kindness and tenderness. He said he had given so much he could give no more, but told her where to go and get the money, and asked Mrs. C., who accompanied me, to assist her, which she did.

The President was seated at his desk. Mrs. C. said to him: "This is Sojourner Truth, who has come all the way

[From Francis B. Carpenter, *Six Months at the White House with Abraham Lincoln*, New York, 1866]

from Michigan to see you." He then arose, gave me his hand, made a bow, and said: "I am pleased to see you."

I said to him: "Mr. President, when you first took your seat I feared you would be torn to pieces, for I likened you unto Daniel, who was thrown into the lions' den; and if the lions did not tear you into pieces, I know that it would be God that had served you; and I said if He spared me I would see you before the four years expired, and He has done so, and now I am here to see you for myself."

He then congratulated me on my having been spared. Then I said: "I appreciate you, for you are the best President who has ever taken the seat." He replied thus: "I expect you have reference to my having emancipated the slaves in my proclamation, but," said he, mentioning the names of several of his predecessors (and among them emphatically that of Washington), "they were all just as good, and would have done just as I have done if the time had come. If the people over the river (pointing across the Potomac) had behaved themselves, I could not have done what I have; but they did not, and I was compelled to do these things." I then said: "I thank God that you were the instrument selected by Him and the people to do it."

He then showed me the Bible presented to him by the colored people of Baltimore. . . . After I had looked it over, I said to him: "This is beautiful indeed; the colored people have given this to the Head of the Government, and that Government once sanctioned laws that would not permit its people to learn enough to enable them to read this Book. And for what? Let them answer who can."

I must say, and I am proud to say, that I never was treated by any one with more kindness and cordiality than was shown me by the great and good man, Abraham Lincoln, by the grace of God President of the United

States for four years more. He took my little book, and with the same hand that signed the death-warrant of slavery, he wrote as follows:—

"For Aunty Sojourner Truth,

"Oct. 29, 1864.

A. Lincoln."

As I was taking my leave, he arose and took my hand, and said he would be pleased to have me call again. I felt that I was in the presence of a friend, and I now thank God from the bottom of my heart that I always advocated his cause, and have done it openly and boldly. I shall feel still more in duty bound to do so in time to come. May God assist me.

Lincoln showing Sojourner Truth the Bible presented by the colored people of Baltimore

"A sweet little rose-bud"

A. E. Andrews records these kind words spoken by Lincoln to a little girl.

AT ONE of the stopping places of the train, a very beautiful little child, having a bouquet of rose-buds in her hand, was lifted up to an open window of the President's car. With a childish lisp she said: "Flowrth for the President!"

The President stepped to the window, took the rose-buds, bent down and kissed the child saying:

"You're a sweet little rose-bud yourself. I hope your life will open into perpetual beauty and goodness."

[From Allen Thorndike Rice, ed., *Reminiscences of Abraham Lincoln by Distinguished Men of His Time*, New York, 1886]

"One good and true friend"

This account of Lincoln's kindness to a poor orphan boy was published in Six Months at the White House.

AMONG a large number of persons waiting in the room to speak with Mr. Lincoln, on a certain day in November, '64, was a small, pale, delicate-looking boy about thirteen years old. The President saw him standing, looking feeble and faint, and said: "Come here, my boy, and tell me what you want." The boy advanced, placed his hand on the arm of the President's chair, and with bowed head and timid accents said: "Mr. President, I have been a drummer in a regiment for two years, and my colonel got angry with me and turned me off. I was taken sick, and have been a long time in hospital. This is the first time I have been out, and I came to see if you could not do something for me." The President looked at him kindly and tenderly, and asked him where he lived. "I have no home," answered the boy. "Where is your father?" "He died in the army," was the reply. "Where is your mother?" continued the President. "My mother is dead also. I have no mother, no father, no brothers, no sisters, and," bursting into tears, "no friends—nobody cares for me." Mr. Lincoln's eyes filled

[From Francis B. Carpenter, *Six Months at the White House with Abraham Lincoln*, New York, 1866]

with tears, and he said to him, "Can't you sell newspapers?" "No," said the boy, "I am too weak; and the surgeon of the hospital told me I must leave, and I have no money, and no place to go to." The scene was wonderfully affecting. The president drew forth a card, and addressing on it certain officials to whom his request was law, gave special directions "to care for this poor boy." The wan face of the little drummer lit up with a happy smile as he received the paper, and he went away convinced that he had one good and true friend, at least in the person of the President.

Thomas Nast's woodcut of "Lincoln and the Little Orphan Boy"

"All the boys . . . are for you"

This recollection was written by William Agnew Paton who, as a young boy, went to the White House to see the President.

ONE OF the most vivid and inspiring memories of my boyhood is of my interview with Abraham Lincoln in October, 1862.

I, a lad going on fourteen years of age, called at the Executive Mansion in Washington and handed to the doorkeeper a card which I had caused to be written especially for use on what was for me a very great occasion by the expert "calligraphist," as he called himself, of Willard's Hotel. Beneath my name, which the card-writer had inscribed with elaborate if not altogether appropriate flourishes, I had appended in my own schoolboy hand-writing, "Nephew of Dr. Cornelius Rea Agnew." My uncle was well known to Mr. Lincoln and thus use of his name doubtless facilitated my admission to the office of the private secretary to the President, where I found the chief magistrate of my country at a desk in conversation with a gentleman, the only other occupant of the room, who was, as I afterward learned, the Minister of France. When I entered the office the President was seated in a curiously constructed

[From William Agnew Paton, "The Card That Brought an Interview," *Century* magazine, December 1913]

armchair made after a design suggested by himself. The
left arm of this unique piece of furniture began low and,
rising in a spiral to form the back, terminated on the right
side of the seat at the height of the shoulders of the person
seated thereon. Mr. Lincoln had placed himself crosswise
in this chair with his long legs hanging over its lower arm,
his back supported by the higher side. When the attendant who had presented my card to the President, and
had then ushered me into the secretary's office, closed the
door behind me and I found myself actually in the presence of Abraham Lincoln, I had the grace to feel embarrassed, for then I realized that I, a mere schoolboy, was
intruding upon the patience and good-nature of a very
busy overwrought man, the great and honored President
of a country in the agony of a civil war. Noting my hesitation, Mr. Lincoln very gently said: "Come in, my son."
Then he arose, disentangling himself, as it were, from the
chair, advanced to meet me, and it seemed to me that I
had never beheld so tall a man, so dignified and impressive
a personage, and certainly I had never felt so small, so in-
significant, "so unpardonably young." As we met, the
President gave me his hand, smiled down upon me, and,
playing upon the similarity in the sound of my name with
that of the person to whom he was about to refer, lightly
asked: "Are you Bailey Peyton, the rebel guerilla we captured the other day?" I stammered an incoherent dis-
claimer of any relationship with the famous Confederate
free-lance, of whose exploits and recent capture the newspapers had much to say. Mr. Lincoln asked me if my uncle
was well and charged me to deliver a kind message to my
kinsman when I returned home to New York. Then, laying
his hand upon my head, he said (how well I remember his
words!) "You come of good people, you will soon be a

grown man. Be a good man. Be a good American. Our country may have need of your services some day."

I had thought up a little speech to deliver when I met the President whom I had been taught to love and revere, but when I stood before him, felt his hand on my head, heard his voice, looked up into his wonderfully expressive, kindly eyes, my emotions were so deeply stirred that I could but smile through tears, and dared only to take his hand, which had dropped from my head, and press it. I looked down abashed, not knowing what to say or do. Mr. Lincoln, evidently noting my confusion, placed his hand on my shoulder and drew me to him, saying, "What can I do for you, sonny?" Encouraged and heartened by his kindly manner, his sympathetic tone of voice, my eyes sought his again and I managed to blurt out: "Mr. Lincoln, all the boys in my school are for you." His smile broadened, he seemed much amused. Then I remember very distinctly the troubled, weary, careworn expression that passed over his face as he replied: "I wish everybody, Congress, all the people, were like you boys." I could say nothing, could only gaze into his benevolent eyes that seemed to look into my very heart. Presently he asked me how old I was, where I went to school, and a few other questions of like familiar sort. And then again, giving me his hand he said: "Now, you must excuse me; I have important business with this gentleman," indicating the personage with whom he had been conversing when I entered the room. I shook hands with the President, turned and walked to the door, faced about, made my manners, as he, reseating himself in the curious armchair, resumed his interview with the minister of France.

I passed from the room and never again saw that wonderful, kindly face until as one of thousands upon thou-

sands of grief-stricken, almost heart-broken fellow coun-
trymen, I passed by his open coffin and beheld for a moment the body of "the murdered President" as it lay in
state in the rotunda of the city hall of my native New
York.

Through all the years that have passed since I stood in
the living presence of the great leader of my people and he
laid his hand gently on my head my memory has held an
undimmed, imperishable picture of the good and kindly
man, the war-worn, overwrought President, who, in the
unbounded goodness of his heart, turned from his work,
his crowding duties, forgetting for a few brief moments his
cruel anxieties, to treat with sweet patience and speak
gently to a schoolboy who had no claim on his attention
and courtesy save that the boy was growing up to be an
American citizen, one of the multitude of "the plain people" of whom Lincoln himself quaintly said: "the good
Lord must love them, he made so many of them." This incident of my boyhood, this great event of my life, of all
events the most memorable and inspiring, this meeting
with Abraham Lincoln was altogether charming. The
memory of it is to me inexpressibly sacred.

When I recall vividly, as I do, the form and face of
Abraham Lincoln as it appeared to my young eyes, I can
appreciate the significance of a remark made to me by Au-
gustus Saint-Gaudens, as he stood modelling "the Chicago
Lincoln": "When I began this work I despaired of making
a worthy or satisfactory statue. So many, almost all, of the
likenesses of Lincoln represent him as ungainly, uncouth,
homely, unpicturesque; but when I had made a study of
his life, had learned more and more of his character, of his
natural nobility and lovableness, his deep and true human
sympathy, had read of him, talked of him with men who

knew him and loved him, I became more and more convinced that his face must have been the most truly beautiful of all I have tried to model." As my good friend the great sculptor created his mind-picture of Abraham Lincoln which he realized in his masterpiece, so I recall to mind his face and form after all the years that have passed since I, a small boy, stood in the living presence of the greatest of Americans. As I think of him now, his greatness of spirit, his worth, integrity, honesty of purpose, his kindliness, his wit and wisdom, his patience—all shone in his countenance and through his wonderful eyes and, as the man was altogether lovable and admirable in the highest sense, I believe that the face that smiled down upon me years ago was in the highest sense beautiful. That I am justified in my belief there is the testimony of his private secretary and co-biographer, Honorable J. G. Nicolay, who says of him: "There was neither oddity, eccentricity, awkwardness, or grotesqueness in his face, figure or movement"; and men and women who knew Lincoln remember his "soft, tender, dreamy, patient, loving eyes—the kindest ever placed in mortal head." And to his wisdom, his genius, his inestimable greatness of spirit, "his nobly humane simplicity of character," there is no need to speak.

"A spirit of frankness and sincerity"

Thomas S. Hopkins reflects on how the great figure of the president influenced his life.

I WAS a country boy of sixteen when the Civil War broke out in 1861. I wanted to enlist, but my parents would not consent. I was persistent in my appeals to them. This continued for a year, and the war went on. Great battles were fought, and some of my older schoolmates were wounded and some were killed. I was nearly beside myself, and finally in June, 1862, my mother, giving way to the thought that perhaps duty was calling, yielded, and I was soon drilling with a new regiment under the shadow of the State House. . . . Before the year had closed I was in a hospital with a gunshot wound.

My first view of Mr. Lincoln was soon after the battle of Antietam, in the fall of 1862. Mr. Lincoln had come to review the Army of the Potomac. Our regiment had marched a long distance in the early morning to reach the reviewing field and then came a long, long wait. I was tired, hungry, and thirsty. But finally there came the sound of bugles and loud cries of "Attention!" from officers. A cloud of dust swept toward us from far down the

[From Thomas S. Hopkins, "A Boy's Recollections of Mr. Lincoln," *St. Nicholas*, May 1922]

line, and out of it gradually emerged a great number of field and staff-officers, their horses galloping rapidly. At the head rode Major General George B. McClellan, and at his side a civilian, dressed in black and wearing a high silk hat. The contrast between the latter and those who were attired in all that glittering panoply of war was striking. In the passing glimpse that I obtained, about all that could be observed was that Mr. Lincoln was very tall and rode his horse with wonderful ease. But in the fraction of the moment that my eyes rested on Mr. Lincoln, somehow my heart warmed toward the great man, and I whispered softly to myself: "I'm glad I enlisted!"

After fourteen months at the front, I was sent to a hospital in Washington. The next time I saw Mr. Lincoln was on the steps of the White House, one evening late in 1863. Mr. Lincoln came out of the front entrance and entered a carriage to be driven to his summer cottage at the Soldiers' Home outside of the city. This was a close-range view.

My father, in eating an apple, had the rather unusual habit of holding it in both hands. Mr. Lincoln, as he stepped out on the portico of the White House, was eating an apple which *he was holding in both hands*! He had on the inevitable high hat, which he wore summer and winter. Still eating the apple, he passed down the steps, bowing and smiling, and entered the closed carriage. He had to bend his tall body very much before he could enter.

The thing that I remember best and care most to remember was the smile that flitted across Mr. Lincoln's plain and rugged face. It was not forced. It was as spontaneous as the smile of a mother looking down into the face of the child in her arms. . . . But there was nothing about him that was imposing or awesome; no exhibition of the pride or arrogance, or even the reserve, that sometimes characterizes the attitudes of rulers of great nations. . . . My boy's heart warmed toward him, and I longed to hear him speak.

Having become unfit for service at the front, I was detailed for duty in the War Department. From that time on I saw Mr. Lincoln almost daily. Many times I saw him driving to or from his summer home, and usually he was followed by a body-guard of cavalry, with long lances at the ends of which fluttered tiny red flags. Frequently, after dinner, Mr. and Mrs. Lincoln drove for pleasure through the streets and parks. Sometimes the President walked, but not often. I heard him address regiments returning from the front, attended receptions at the White House and took the great man's hand. Later in the evening, Mr. and Mrs. Lincoln would come into the spacious East Room for a few moments. It was a brilliant spectacle for a country boy to witness. The great men of the nation— those high in official life, diplomats from foreign countries in court dress and bedecked with brilliant decorations, generals of the army in full uniform—and ladies young and old, wearing such beautiful costumes and adorned with such glittering diamonds as I had never dreamed of, were there, and excited my wonder. The crush was so great that the system of checking wraps, etc., frequently got out of hand; and on one of these occasions, I lost my hat and was forced much to my chagrin, to escort a very sweet girl home with no covering for my head. The girl forgave me, and later, to emphasize the fact, married me; but she still teases me about it.

I will never forget the last time I saw this greatest of men. It was on Friday evening of April 14th, 1865. That evening, just before sunset, a companion and I were walking near the Navy Yard entrance, when Mr. and Mrs. Lincoln passed in the White House carriage, evidently intending to drive through the Navy Yard grounds. The usual mounted body-guard was not in attendance. It was because of the absence of any guard, perhaps, that my companion and I stopped and watched them pass. The lines in the President's face had deepened and lengthened. Otherwise it was little changed. It had not hardened. Rather it had softened and mellowed as does the face of one who has come through great tribulation with faith undimmed. I turned to my companion and said: "There is no other country in the civilized world where one may see the ruler of a great people riding on the streets with no guard or escort."

Four hours later Mr. Lincoln was mortally wounded. It was a wild night in Washington. From Winder's Building, signal-lights were constantly flashing; from the circle of great forts that surrounded and protected the capital city could be heard the drums beating the long roll; squadrons of cavalry dashed through the streets, scabbards clanged against stirrups, and horses' steel shoes pounded the pavements; the streets downtown were crowded with excited, gesticulating men, some of whom were swearing who never swore before; and some, to whom tears hitherto had been unknown, were crying, while a mob filled Tenth Street and the house across the way into which Mr. Lincoln had been carried. I was on the streets all night, going from point to point, gathering such news as I could, while my heart was heavy. . . .

In the early morning, the soul of that greatest and noblest of men took its flight, leaving behind a heart-broken nation. Even the heavens wept, for all day long steadily the rain fell. I next saw Mr. Lincoln in his casket as he lay in the White House. A guard of honor, immovable as statues, surrounded him. Tears clouded my vision as I looked for the last time upon that face which in death seemed, if possible, nobler than in life. Four days afterward, Mr. Lincoln's body was borne down Pennsylvania Avenue to the railroad station. All Washington was there, silent and grief-stricken. I have seen all the great historic processions for which that avenue is noted, since Mr. Lincoln's second inauguration—the Grand Review of 1865; the return of the Spanish War and World War veterans, the inauguration of all the Presidents—but in solemnity, in the depth of feeling stirred up in the hearts of the people, in historic significance, nothing that compared with this. The heavens wept when Lincoln died, but on this day Nature smiled her sweetest. The sun shone brightly, the air was balmy; the birds sang, and it seemed as if Nature were trying to comfort a stricken people.

More than half a century has passed and I am now an old man. I have seen mighty events occur in the world's history, and in a very humble way have participated in some of them. I look back on a life of great activity, but there is nothing I recall in all the years since childhood, except the memory of my mother, that brings such satisfaction as the fact that I saw Mr. Lincoln many times and actually took his hand and spoke to him. Somehow, when as a boy I saw and heard the great man whom so many writers described as uncouth, I did not think him awkward or ungraceful. Instead, such a kindly light shone forth from those deep-set eyes, there was such friendliness in that gentle smile, and there was such a spirit of frankness and sincerity in every feature, almost any discerning man or boy might have seen that here was a man who loved his fellow man, and that in him dwelt the spirit of the Divine Master.

Secretary of War, Edwin Stanton, standing by Lincoln's bed when he died, closed the eyes of the great leader, and uttered this simple yet poignant phrase:

"There lies a man for the ages."

Index

St. Louis, Mo., 18, 19, 21
Stanton, Edwin, 9, 11, 47, 120
Stanton, Rev. Robert Livingston, 27
Stanton, Robert Brewster, 27–31
Stuart, Gen. J. E. B., 66

Truth, Sojourner, 103–105

Union League of Chicago, 84

Van Buren, John D., 22–25
Van Santwood, Rev. Cornelius, 36
Vandersloot, Louisa, 70–71

Weed, Samuel R., 19–21
White House, 10, 15, 49, 51, 84, 115
Willard's Hotel, 53, 88, 109
Wilson, Henry, 12
Wormley's Hotel, 22

10/02 (7) 5/02.
2/06 (15) 1/05.
7/16 (24) 1/15